AF094451

The History of North Korea

CRAFTED BY SKRIUWER

Copyright © 2025 by Skriuwer.

All rights reserved. No part of this book may be used or reproduced in any form whatsoever without written permission except in the case of brief quotations in critical articles or reviews.

At **Skriuwer**, we're more than just a team—we're a global community of people who love books. In Frisian, "Skriuwer" means "writer," and that's at the heart of what we do: creating and sharing books with readers worldwide. Wherever you are in the world, **Skriuwer** is here to inspire learning.

Frisian is one of the oldest languages in Europe, closely related to English and Dutch, and is spoken by about **500,000 people** in the province of **Friesland** (Fryslân), located in the northern Netherlands. It's the second official language of the Netherlands, but like many minority languages, Frisian faces the challenge of survival in a modern, globalized world.

We're using the money we earn to promote the Frisian language.

For more information, contact : **kontakt@skriuwer.com** (www.skriuwer.com)

Disclaimer:
The images in this book are creative reinterpretations of historical scenes. While every effort was made to accurately capture the essence of the periods depicted, some illustrations may include artistic embellishments or approximations. They are intended to evoke the atmosphere and spirit of the times rather than serve as precise historical records.

TABLE OF CONTENTS

CHAPTER 1: EARLY SETTLEMENTS ON THE KOREAN PENINSULA

- *Geography's influence on ancient life and survival.*
- *First farming practices and the rise of small villages.*
- *Spiritual beliefs and myths shaping early culture.*

CHAPTER 2: THE RISE OF EARLY KINGDOMS IN THE NORTH

- *Formation of tribal federations into larger political entities.*
- *Legend of Dangun and the symbolism of Gojoseon.*
- *Goguryeo's early expansion and conflicts with neighboring states.*

CHAPTER 3: THE GORYEO DYNASTY AND NORTHERN TERRITORIES

- *Wang Geon's unification and the establishment of Goryeo.*
- *Defense and administration in northern frontier regions.*
- *Cultural and religious developments under Goryeo rule.*

CHAPTER 4: THE JOSEON DYNASTY'S INFLUENCE ON NORTHERN REGIONS

- *Neo-Confucian governance and its impact on local life.*
- *Military garrisons and border management in the north.*
- *Cultural shifts and the evolving social hierarchy.*

CHAPTER 5: FOREIGN INVASIONS AND CHANGES IN POWER

- *Japan's invasion (Imjin War) and its aftermath.*
- *Manchu invasions and Joseon's tributes to Qing.*
- *Lessons learned and the kingdom's internal reorganization.*

CHAPTER 6: THE LATE JOSEON PERIOD AND SHIFTS IN SOCIETY

- *Reforms under kings Yeongjo and Jeongjo.*
- *Agricultural improvements and social tensions.*
- *Neo-Confucian values versus emerging new ideas.*

CHAPTER 7: EARLY FOREIGN INFLUENCES AND KOREA'S OPENING

- *Increasing Western presence and maritime incidents.*
- *Ganghwa Treaty and forced trade with Japan.*
- *Modernization efforts and conflicts over isolation.*

CHAPTER 8: JAPANESE OCCUPATION (1910–1945)

- *Loss of sovereignty and harsh colonial policies.*
- *Cultural suppression and economic exploitation by Japan.*
- *Seeds of resistance movements taking root.*

CHAPTER 9: GROWING NATIONALISM AND RESISTANCE MOVEMENTS

- *March First Movement and its lasting influence.*
- *Formation of underground groups and independence fighters.*
- *Cultural nationalism fostering a sense of collective identity.*

CHAPTER 10: THE END OF WORLD WAR II AND THE DIVISION OF KOREA

- *Japan's surrender and the sudden power vacuum.*
- *Soviet and American occupations leading to the 38th Parallel split.*
- *Formation of separate governments in the north and south.*

CHAPTER 11: THE BIRTH OF NORTH KOREA (DPRK)

- Early governance under Soviet guidance.
- Land reforms, nationalization of industry, and social restructuring.
- Kim Il Sung's rise as the central figure of the new state.

CHAPTER 12: KIM IL SUNG'S EARLY LEADERSHIP

- Consolidation of power and elimination of rival factions.
- Cult of personality expanding around the Great Leader.
- Steps toward conflict with the south foreshadowing the Korean War.

CHAPTER 13: THE KOREAN WAR (1950–1953)

- Northern invasion and rapid early advances.
- UN intervention, Chinese involvement, and bloody stalemate.
- Armistice and the legacy of devastation on the peninsula.

CHAPTER 14: REBUILDING AFTER THE WAR

- Post-war reconstruction campaigns and volunteer labor.
- Industrial and agricultural revival under strict central planning.
- Kim Il Sung's continued consolidation through economic successes.

CHAPTER 15: JUCHE IDEOLOGY AND ITS IMPACT

- Origins of self-reliance principles and their formal adoption.
- Shaping politics, economy, and culture around Juche.
- Strengthening Kim Il Sung's personality cult and national identity.

CHAPTER 16: ECONOMIC PLANS AND INDUSTRIAL CHANGES

- *State-led five-year and seven-year plans focusing on heavy industry.*
- *Collectivized farming challenges and shortages of consumer goods.*
- *Dependence on foreign socialist allies and emerging debt issues.*

CHAPTER 17: CULTURAL AND SOCIAL SHIFTS UNDER KIM IL SUNG

- *Control of religion, education, and family life.*
- *Promotion of revolutionary arts and mass cultural events.*
- *Social frameworks reinforcing loyalty and model citizen ideals.*

CHAPTER 18: LATER YEARS OF KIM IL SUNG'S RULE

- *Deepening personality cult and preparing Kim Jong Il as successor.*
- *Strains from the Soviet bloc collapse and economic stagnation.*
- *Diplomatic maneuvers and continued isolation despite global changes.*

CHAPTER 19: CHALLENGES BEFORE THE MODERN ERA

- *Transition to Kim Jong Il's leadership after 1994.*
- *Arduous March famine crisis and coping through unofficial markets.*
- *Nuclear disputes rising and the struggle for survival in the 1990s.*

CHAPTER 20: STEPS TOWARD THE FUTURE

- *Legacy of resilience vs. isolation in the new century.*
- *Subtle economic adaptations and the ongoing Kim family rule.*
- *Reflections on history's influence on North Korea's path forward.*

CHAPTER 1

EARLY SETTLEMENTS ON THE KOREAN PENINSULA

Introduction

The history of North Korea begins with the story of ancient peoples on the Korean Peninsula. Long before there were clear divisions between north and south, groups of settlers built small villages, practiced farming, and hunted animals in valleys and mountains. Over a long period, these early societies grew and changed, forming unique cultures and local traditions. In this chapter, we will look at how these first communities came into being, where they lived, and what their daily lives might have been like. We will also see how geography played an important role in shaping their habits and customs. This background is essential to understand how later kingdoms arose in the northern part of the peninsula.

1.1 The Land and Its Influence

The northern region of the Korean Peninsula is known for its rough terrain, with tall mountains and deep valleys. Winters are harsh and cold, while summers are shorter and can be quite wet. Rivers like the Yalu (Amnok) and the Tumen flow through the north, making borders with neighboring lands. This geography greatly affected how people lived in ancient times.

Early settlers in the north faced challenges due to these natural conditions. They had to find ways to keep warm in cold winters, and they also had to plan their agriculture around shorter growing seasons. Some groups settled near rivers, which gave them a steady supply of water for farming. Others moved into mountain valleys, where they could hunt wild animals and gather local plants.

Because of this environment, early people learned to be resourceful. They built shelters using wood, mud, and stone. They wove clothes from hemp or other local fibers. They also learned to store food so that they could survive through long winters. All these skills, formed in ancient times, set the stage for the cultures that developed later in the north.

1.2 Ancient Tools and Artifacts

Archaeologists have found many clues about these early communities by digging up pottery, stone tools, and bones. These artifacts tell us a lot about what life might have been like thousands of years ago:

- **Pottery**: Early pottery from these settlements shows simple designs. Pots were usually made by hand and then fired in open pits or simple kilns. People used these pots to store grains or water.
- **Stone Tools**: Axes, arrowheads, and knives were made from different types of stone. Over time, tool-making improved, allowing people to hunt more effectively and clear land for farming.
- **Bone and Shell Ornaments**: Some settlers also made ornaments from animal bones or shells. These items might have been used for decoration or for spiritual purposes.

These artifacts prove that ancient peoples in the north were skilled at using local materials. They knew how to adapt to their environment. Their knowledge in crafting tools laid the groundwork for more advanced technology in later periods.

1.3 Early Farming and Gathering

Farming in ancient North Korea was not easy. The colder climate and rugged land made large-scale agriculture a challenge. Still, these early settlers learned to grow grains like millet and barley. They may also have grown beans and other local crops that could handle cooler temperatures. Hunting and gathering remained vital. People hunted deer, boar, and smaller animals, while they gathered nuts, berries, and wild vegetables in nearby forests.

Why Farming Was Important

1. It provided a steady food source when hunting was scarce.
2. It allowed groups to settle in one place, leading to more stable communities.
3. It promoted trade between neighboring settlements, as some areas were better for growing certain crops than others.

Over many generations, farming practices became more advanced. People created simple irrigation methods near riverbanks, which helped them water crops. They also rotated fields or left some land fallow to keep the soil healthy. These improvements in farming led to population growth and the start of small village communities.

1.4 The Growth of Villages

As farming became more reliable, people stopped moving around as much. They formed permanent villages or clusters of homes. Houses were often built close together for protection. Villagers cooperated to build walls or fences to keep out wild animals and to keep their livestock safe.

In some communities, there might have been simple forms of leadership. A respected elder or a group of elders decided how to share water, how to settle disagreements, and how to plan for winter. Over time, these early leaders might have developed into more formal tribal heads.

Daily Life in Early Villages

- People woke up early to tend to crops or go hunting.
- Women and men shared tasks. Women often managed food storage and some farm tasks, while men often focused on hunting or heavy labor.
- Children learned from parents and elders, helping with small tasks until they were old enough to do bigger jobs.
- Evenings were for storytelling and possibly sharing spiritual or cultural traditions.

This village life made people stronger as a community, taught them to rely on each other, and helped them pass down traditions. It was an important step before the rise of more structured societies and kingdoms.

1.5 Spiritual Beliefs and Community Rituals

We do not have written records from these ancient times. However, artifacts like simple altars, decorated pottery, and burial sites suggest that early settlers had spiritual beliefs. They might have worshipped nature, such as the sun, the moon, or local spirits they believed lived in rivers and mountains. Some communities held rituals to pray for good harvests or to honor their ancestors.

Burial Customs

- **Simple Tombs**: Many people were buried with small items, like pottery or stone tools.
- **Burial Mounds**: In some areas, more important members of a community were buried in low mounds.
- **Burial Gifts**: Items found beside the remains suggest early beliefs in an afterlife, or at least a respect for the dead.

These spiritual practices gave people hope and a sense of unity. Ceremonies or festivals might have been tied to the farming cycle, such as planting or harvest times. Over centuries, these shared beliefs and rituals would evolve into more structured religions and cultural traditions.

1.6 Interaction Between Groups

No village existed on its own. People traveled to trade goods they needed, like salt, certain minerals, or crops not grown in their own area. This meant that even at an early stage, there was some connection between communities. Traveling might have been dangerous due to wild animals or harsh weather, but the need for trade pushed people to find safe routes.

Trade and exchange also helped spread ideas, customs, and even technology. One group might learn a new way of farming or a different style of pottery from another group. Over time, these exchanges paved the way for a shared cultural identity across the peninsula, though each region, including the north, kept its own local uniqueness.

1.7 Development of Early Social Structures

As villages grew, people began to specialize. Some became skilled hunters, others were better at making pottery or tools, and some learned how to lead rituals or give spiritual advice. This specialization slowly shaped social structures:

1. **Leaders or Elders**: Managed village affairs and solved disputes.
2. **Skilled Workers**: Craftsmen who made items such as tools, pottery, or simple clothes.
3. **Hunters/Farmers**: Provided food for the community.
4. **Spiritual Figures**: Led ceremonies, offered guidance, and taught community values.

While we cannot say these positions were as rigid as in later kingdoms, there is evidence of different roles among the people. These roles helped each community function more smoothly. Over long periods, some leaders or families might have gained extra influence or wealth, laying the roots of future hierarchical systems.

1.8 The Legend of Dangun and Ancient Korean Myths

A famous story in Korean tradition is the Legend of Dangun, who is said to have founded the first Korean kingdom called Gojoseon (though its center was not necessarily in the far north as we know it today). While this legend is more linked to the central or northern parts of the peninsula, it also influences how later eras viewed the region's past. Even though the exact historical truth behind these myths is debated, they show that ancient Koreans believed in a shared ancestry and that the land had divine roots.

For the north, stories like these and other local myths would have shaped people's ideas about their homeland. Myths about mountains, rivers, and local heroes gave villagers a sense of identity. Over time, rulers and leaders used these myths to claim they were chosen by the heavens or by ancestors to lead.

1.9 Transition to Larger Communities

As centuries passed, some villages in the north joined together for better defense and sharing of resources. This might have been the start of small tribal federations. They protected each other from raids, worked together on larger projects like digging irrigation channels, or pooled labor to build stronger walls.

These cooperations showed the beginnings of structured societies that would later grow into city-states or early kingdoms. Though we do not have clear historical records from this time, we can guess that these alliances laid the groundwork for the more famous early kingdoms in the region.

1.10 Influence from Neighboring Regions

Early people in the north did not live in isolation. Historical evidence suggests that tribes near the northern borders traded with groups in Manchuria (a region to the north of Korea). Through this contact, they might have learned new ways of making bronze tools when the Bronze Age began.

Bronze Age Changes

- Stronger metal tools improved farming and hunting.
- Bronze weapons made conflicts more serious and let some groups dominate others.
- Bronze items were a symbol of wealth or power, so communities that had them might have gained higher status.

This move into the Bronze Age marked a key turning point. Societies that embraced bronze gained advantages in both warfare and daily life. Their influence would stretch far beyond their immediate region.

1.11 The Start of Social Hierarchy

With the introduction of bronze, certain groups or leaders who controlled the production or trade of these metal items became more powerful. This led to noticeable social layers: a leader class (or ruling class), skilled workers who shaped bronze, and common farmers or hunters. Over time, more permanent leadership structures emerged, possibly based around families who held power.

Farming communities that produced surplus food could support more complex societies, including specialized artisans, warriors, and possibly traders who traveled to distant regions. All these new social roles added layers to community structure, making society more complex than the simple village life before.

1.12 The Emergence of Early Fortified Settlements

As groups competed for farmland and resources, fortified settlements started to appear. People built walls or ditches around their homes, sometimes on hilltops or in spots that were easier to defend. These settlements often turned into local centers of power. A leader who controlled a fortified town might demand food or loyalty from nearby villages.

In the north, certain areas with good farmland or mineral resources, such as iron or copper ore, became targets for competing communities. Controlling these resources meant control over better tools and weapons, which then led to more power. This cycle pushed some communities to grow stronger while others weakened.

1.13 Cultural Practices and Artisan Skills

Even in these early times, people did more than just hunt, farm, or fight. They also expressed themselves through art and craft:

- **Bronze Mirrors and Bells**: These items were often decorated with simple patterns. They might have been used in rituals or as symbols of authority.
- **Pottery with Patterns**: Some pottery featured swirling lines or geometric shapes, possibly reflecting local beliefs or aesthetics.
- **Jewelry and Decorations**: Skilled artisans made simple bracelets, rings, and hairpins using bronze or bone.

These creative works show that early people cared about beauty and symbolism, not just survival. As new ideas arrived from neighboring regions, artistic styles grew more diverse, gradually shaping a distinct local culture in the north.

1.14 The Role of Storytelling

Without writing systems in the earliest periods, storytelling was crucial for passing down history and lessons. Elders told tales of heroes, battles, and moral teachings. These stories helped shape a sense of identity, teaching the young about their ancestors' bravery or wisdom.

Some stories might have included warnings about greed or foolishness, showing the values these early people held dear. Others explained natural phenomena like thunderstorms or droughts, attributing them to spirits or gods. Over many years, these oral traditions would evolve, eventually influencing the myths and histories written down in later dynasties.

1.15 Moving Toward Organized Society

By the time we reach the late Bronze Age, we see hints of more centralized organization in the northern parts of the peninsula. Ruling families or clans started forming alliances or waging wars to expand their territory. While this did not yet look like a unified kingdom, we can see the early steps leading to more complex political structures.

Leaders might have collected tributes or taxes from farmers. They used these resources to support warriors and to conduct trade. Skilled artisans who worked with bronze could live under the protection of these leaders, and in return, they supplied the community with weapons, tools, and ceremonial objects. This interdependence among the different members of society showed a more advanced system than the simple villages of the past.

1.16 Challenges in Reconstructing Ancient History

Reconstructing the details of these ancient societies can be difficult. We rely on archaeology and legends because written records from these times do not exist or are extremely scarce. Scholars piece together evidence from tools, artifacts, and the ruins of settlements to make educated guesses.

Still, despite the gaps, we can see clear steps of growth: from roaming groups of hunters to settled villages, from small tribal communities to more structured societies with fortified towns. The unique geography of the north, combined with influences from Manchuria and beyond, led to cultural traits that would later shape the identity of future kingdoms in the region.

Conclusion

The foundation of North Korea's long history rests on the lives of these ancient peoples. They overcame harsh climates, learned to farm, and began shaping the land around them. Their crafts, social structures, and beliefs grew steadily over time. In the next chapter, we will see how these smaller groups started to merge or clash, giving rise to the earliest kingdoms that would strongly influence later North Korean history.

CHAPTER 2

THE RISE OF EARLY KINGDOMS IN THE NORTH

Introduction

After centuries of gradual growth and organization, larger political entities began to appear on the Korean Peninsula. In the northern regions, powerful tribal groups and emerging leaders started to form what we might call early kingdoms. Though records are limited, we know these entities had rulers, armies, and structured societies. One such kingdom was Gojoseon, which many consider the first Korean kingdom. In this chapter, we will discuss how these early kingdoms took shape in the north, the role of expanding trade, and how warfare and alliances set the stage for bigger changes in the centuries to come.

2.1 Moving Beyond Tribal Federations

In the previous chapter, we saw how villages combined to protect themselves and control resources. Over time, these alliances grew stronger and eventually formed the basis of early kingdoms. Tribal federations might have recognized a single paramount chief or king, someone who commanded loyalty through both might and tradition.

Characteristics of Early Kingdoms

1. **Defined Territory**: They claimed specific lands, including farmland and key trade routes.
2. **Central Authority**: A leader or ruling clan had final say over the entire area.
3. **Military Organization**: There were groups of warriors who defended or expanded the kingdom's borders.
4. **Formal Beliefs or Rituals**: Rulers often backed their authority with religious or mythical claims.

These early kingdoms often overlapped with or challenged each other. Because the peninsula was not unified under one government yet, there were many power struggles in the north and in other regions.

2.2 Gojoseon: A Legendary Beginning

One kingdom that stands out in ancient Korean history is Gojoseon. Its founding is often linked to the legendary figure Dangun. While the exact dates and territories are debated, many stories say Gojoseon emerged around the northern parts of the peninsula and parts of what is now Manchuria.

What Made Gojoseon Notable

- It had a recognized king or ruler who governed from a capital city, though the exact location is uncertain.
- It engaged in trade and possibly conflict with surrounding tribes and early states.
- Its influence spread to a wide area, hinting at organized systems for collecting resources and controlling people.

Gojoseon is important because it serves as a symbolic first state in Korean history. Its legends and stories inspired later kingdoms and fed into Korean identity as a proud, ancient civilization.

2.3 Interaction with Chinese States

To understand the rise of early northern kingdoms, we must consider the influence of nearby Chinese states. By this time, China had developed advanced political systems and cultural practices. Kingdoms like Gojoseon likely traded with Chinese regions, bringing in items like silk, iron, or other valuable goods. In return, Chinese texts mention a "Joseon" or "Chaoxian," pointing to the recognition of a northern Korean state.

But these relationships were not always peaceful. The more powerful Chinese states sometimes viewed Gojoseon and its neighbors as threats or as lesser entities to be subdued. Over time, Gojoseon faced invasions and had to defend its territory. These conflicts forced northern rulers to strengthen their military and form alliances, setting the course for further development.

2.4 Growth of Agriculture and Craftsmanship

As these early kingdoms formed, they began to organize farming more efficiently. Rulers saw that well-fed subjects could build stronger armies and support the kingdom's growth. They encouraged better farming tools and, when possible, introduced iron technology for plowing and harvesting. This shift made it easier to produce surplus grain, which the rulers taxed or stored.

Advances in Craftsmanship

- **Iron Tools**: Stronger and more durable than bronze, iron plows and sickles improved farming output.
- **Weapon Making**: Iron swords and arrowheads gave armies a military edge.
- **Building**: Palaces or forts used stronger materials, sometimes stone or advanced wood constructions.

With improved agriculture and crafts, early kingdoms like Gojoseon became more stable and wealthier, able to manage bigger populations and more warriors.

2.5 Trade Routes and Cultural Exchange

Trade expanded during this period, connecting the northern kingdoms with distant regions. Goods such as grains, cloth, or metal items traveled along routes that passed through mountain valleys and river corridors. The existence of trading outposts and markets in these areas helped spread not just goods but also ideas.

Benefits of Trade

1. **Wealth**: Rulers could gather taxes from merchants and local producers.
2. **Culture**: Ideas about religion, technology, and art moved from place to place.
3. **Diplomacy**: Sometimes, trade led to alliances or peace treaties, since both sides profited from open routes.

These commercial interactions laid the groundwork for a more connected world. The northern kingdoms were no longer isolated; they shared in the wider network of East Asia.

2.6 Establishing Early Laws and Governance

With the growth of population and territory, early kingdoms needed some form of law to keep order. Although no formal legal texts remain from Gojoseon's earliest times, later references and archaeological findings suggest that rules and customs were written down or understood orally. Rulers might have had councils of nobles or tribal chiefs who advised them.

Reasons for Laws

- To settle property disputes among farmers and landowners.
- To regulate trade and collect taxes.
- To punish crimes and keep peace within the kingdom.
- To organize public works like road building or defense projects.

In some records, Gojoseon is credited with having a set of laws called the "Eight Prohibitions," although details are vague. Even so, we see a shift toward formal governance, which is a big step from the smaller tribal groups of earlier times.

2.7 Conflicts and the Fall of Gojoseon

As Gojoseon grew, it drew attention from powerful neighbors. Historical accounts mention conflicts with the Han dynasty of China. Around the 2nd century BCE, these tensions led to major battles. Eventually, Han forces overran parts of Gojoseon, leading to its collapse or severe weakening.

Consequences

1. **Han Commanderies**: The Chinese set up commanderies (administrative areas) in the northern Korean Peninsula.
2. **Power Shift**: Local leaders who cooperated with the Han dynasty could gain influence, while others fled or rebelled.
3. **New Local States**: The weakening of Gojoseon allowed smaller states to emerge or expand, such as Buyeo and Goguryeo.

The fall of Gojoseon marks a turning point, but the idea of a northern kingdom remained strong. Over time, new states arose from its legacy.

2.8 Goguryeo and Other Successor States

Not long after Gojoseon's decline, other powers filled the vacuum. Among the most notable was Goguryeo, which began as a small state in the northern region but eventually became one of the Three Kingdoms of Korea. Though Goguryeo's golden era came later, its roots stretch back to this time of chaos and reshuffling.

Other Northern Entities

- **Buyeo**: Located further north, it had cultural ties to Gojoseon. It eventually influenced Goguryeo.
- **Okjeo and Dongye**: Smaller states that existed near the northern and eastern parts of the peninsula.

These early kingdoms each had their own rulers, cultures, and ambitions. They often fought or formed alliances, shaping a complex political landscape in the north.

2.9 Society and Culture in the Early Kingdom Phase

Even during warfare and political change, ordinary people kept farming, making crafts, and practicing their beliefs. Societies in early northern kingdoms likely remained layered. Nobles and warriors held higher ranks, while farmers, craftspeople, and merchants made up the bulk of the population.

Cultural Aspects

- **Religion**: Shamanistic rituals probably continued, with a growing influence from Chinese philosophies like Confucianism in the ruling classes.
- **Clothing**: Simple garments, often made from hemp or wool. Nobles might have worn finer cloth or silk if they had connections to Chinese trade.
- **Architecture**: Wooden houses were common, but palaces or important buildings might have used stone foundations.

Because contact with outside regions was steady, many cultural elements blended into the local traditions, creating a diverse but distinct northern Korean style.

2.10 Rise of Goguryeo: A Snapshot

Goguryeo eventually rose to become a major kingdom, but its earliest roots lie in smaller tribal communities that banded together in the northern border regions. The founding story mentions Jumong, a legendary figure who established Goguryeo. Whether the tales are literal or symbolic, they reflect the hopes of a people seeking a strong leader to unite them.

In its early days, Goguryeo benefited from the decline of Gojoseon and the shifting powers after Han China set up its commanderies. Through military action and alliances, Goguryeo pushed back against the Han commanderies, seizing territory and growing in influence. By the 1st century CE, Goguryeo was on its way to becoming one of the dominant forces in northern Korea and beyond.

2.11 Government and Royal Power

As kingdoms like Goguryeo took shape, the concept of a royal court became clearer. Rulers claimed a divine or semi-divine right to govern. They held ceremonies to show their authority. Courts included advisers, often from noble families, who helped plan military campaigns or manage the kingdom's resources.

Royal Duties

1. **Defense**: Keep enemies away and protect the people.
2. **Administration**: Collect taxes, store food, and maintain roads.
3. **Justice**: Make laws or rulings to solve conflicts.
4. **Religion**: Oversee important rituals, sometimes serving as a bridge between the gods and the people.

These responsibilities gave the king wide-reaching power, but he still needed the support of noble families or influential clans. In many cases, marriage alliances between ruling families helped secure loyalties and prevent internal strife.

2.12 Everyday Life Under Early Kingdoms

For most commoners, life revolved around working the land or practicing a craft. People had to provide taxes or labor to the kingdom. Men could be called up for military service, especially in times of conflict. Women worked at home and in the fields, and they also played roles in markets, selling farm goods or homemade items.

Social Structure

- **Royal Family**: Occupied the top, living in palaces or well-guarded compounds.
- **Nobles/Aristocrats**: Owned land and had peasants working for them. They often held official positions.
- **Commoners**: Farmers, craftsmen, merchants. They could move up if they gained wealth or favor with the court, but this was rare.
- **Slaves or Serfs**: Some people, possibly captured in wars, had very limited rights and worked for nobles or the royal family.

Despite these classes, local communities kept a sense of unity through festivals, religious ceremonies, and shared customs. The identity of being under a single king also gave people a collective sense of belonging.

2.13 The Influence of Ancient Beliefs

Spiritual life in the early kingdoms continued traditions from tribal times. Many people believed in nature spirits, ancestor worship, and the power of shamans—people who communicated with the spirit world. Over time, these beliefs mixed with ideas from Daoism, Confucianism, and even early Buddhism, though Buddhism gained a stronger footing in later centuries.

Rituals and ceremonies were often held to pray for good harvests or victory in battle. Kings sometimes used religion to legitimize their rule, claiming approval from the heavens or from powerful ancestral spirits. This bond between belief and political authority helped shape the culture of early kingdoms in the north.

2.14 Ongoing Conflicts and Shifting Borders

The early kingdoms faced constant challenges from both neighbors in the peninsula and powers from outside, like Chinese dynasties or nomadic tribes in Manchuria. Borders were not fixed. A stretch of land might be captured by one kingdom and then retaken by another in a matter of years.

Impact on Populations

- People living near border areas often moved if the land changed hands, seeking safer regions.
- Rulers built fortresses along strategic points to guard rivers, mountain passes, or trade routes.
- Diplomacy was sometimes practiced, but many alliances were unstable, leading to frequent fighting.

This turbulent environment forced northern rulers to be vigilant, shaping them into more military-minded leaders who sought to fortify their kingdoms at all costs.

2.15 The Cultural Legacy of the North

Even though different kingdoms rose and fell, the northern region built a heritage of strong, independent states that influenced later Korean history. Gojoseon's example paved the way for Goguryeo and others to claim they were rightful heirs to an old kingdom. This sense of historical pride sometimes became a tool for uniting people or justifying expansion.

Art, pottery, and burial customs from the north also left their mark. Early kingdom tombs sometimes contained intricate items or paintings reflecting daily life and beliefs. While many of these tombs belong to the later Goguryeo period, their roots lie in earlier practices.

2.16 Society's Adaptability

One reason these northern kingdoms could survive was their adaptability. They were open to learning military techniques, adopting new farming methods, or borrowing governing ideas that worked well for larger populations. This blend of tradition and innovation allowed them to keep pace with changes in the region.

Examples of Adaptability

- Learning how to make better iron weapons from neighboring states or from captured artisans.
- Using some Chinese administrative ideas, like record-keeping or tax systems, while keeping local customs.
- Building alliances through marriage, even with people who once were enemies.

This practical approach helped the northern kingdoms remain vital players in the region's shifting power balance.

2.17 Long-Term Effects of Early Kingdoms

Although many details of the early kingdoms are lost, their imprint on history is clear. They established patterns of governance, social hierarchy, and cultural identity that shaped later dynasties on the Korean Peninsula. For North Korea in particular, the memory of these ancient states ties into a long-held narrative of a distinct northern lineage.

Moreover, the early kingdoms set the stage for the well-known Three Kingdoms period (Goguryeo, Baekje, and Silla), which would dominate Korean history in the centuries ahead. By focusing on the northern perspective, we see how these states were not just footnotes, but essential parts of Korea's story.

2.20 Conclusion and Transition

The rise of early kingdoms in the north is a story of growth, conflict, and resilience. Gojoseon laid a legendary foundation, and while it eventually fell, its legacy continued through successor states like Goguryeo. These entities showed strong organization, a willingness to adopt new ideas, and a deep cultural heritage. In the next chapters, we will explore how these kingdoms, especially Goguryeo, evolved and influenced the northern region's destiny.

The lessons from these early kingdoms—cooperation, strategic defense, and cultural exchange—would guide the next stages of North Korean history. As we move forward in time, we will see how Goguryeo rose to power, faced off with powerful Chinese dynasties, and shaped the identity of the northern people in lasting ways.

CHAPTER 3

THE GORYEO DYNASTY AND NORTHERN TERRITORIES

Introduction

The Goryeo Dynasty lasted from 918 to 1392. It was a very important period for the entire Korean Peninsula. After the earlier kingdoms went through many wars and changes, a man named Wang Geon established a new dynasty. This dynasty took control of lands in both the south and north, bringing together many different people under one rule. During Goryeo, the northern territories played a key role in defense and in cultural exchange. Many outside groups, like the Khitan and the Jurchen, lived beyond the northern borders, leading to conflict and trade. Also, Buddhism grew strong during this period, shaping art, society, and daily life across the kingdom, including in the north.

In this chapter, we will explore how Goryeo began, how it treated its northern regions, and how the north changed through times of war and peace. We will learn about trade, religion, government systems, and the everyday lives of people who called the northern part of Goryeo home. By studying these details, we gain a clearer picture of how history in the north continued to develop and set the stage for later periods.

3.1 Founding of Goryeo

Goryeo rose from a time of confusion known as the Later Three Kingdoms period (late 9th to early 10th centuries). After the decline of Unified Silla, several local lords and warlords fought to control land. Wang Geon was among these figures. He came from a city called Songak, which later became Gaegyeong (also called Kaesong).

Wang Geon was skilled in both war and diplomacy. He formed alliances with powerful families in the north and south. He also showed mercy to conquered enemies, which made it easier for people to accept his rule. In 918, Wang Geon established the new kingdom, naming it Goryeo, a word linked to the old Goguryeo. By picking this name, he showed his wish to connect with the famous northern kingdom of past centuries.

One of Wang Geon's main goals was unifying the peninsula. This task was not easy, but by 935, Goryeo had ended the rule of Later Baekje and Unified Silla, bringing most of the land under its authority. The capital was set in Gaegyeong, a city that sat in a more northern spot than some older capitals. This choice reminded everyone that Goryeo claimed the heritage of Goguryeo.

3.2 Early Control of the Northern Lands

When Goryeo formed, the northern lands were not fully secure. Various tribal groups and smaller states, such as the Jurchen, lived beyond Goryeo's boundary. In some places, there were still influences from Balhae, a state that existed to the north after Goguryeo's fall. Balhae itself had recently collapsed due to attacks from the Khitan people (of the Liao Dynasty).

Wang Geon and his early successors saw the north as both a shield and a doorway. It was a shield against northern invaders, but it was also a doorway for trade with people in Manchuria and beyond. Goryeo rulers hoped to reclaim territories that once belonged to Goguryeo, though they faced many challenges.

To strengthen their position, Goryeo kings built forts, watchtowers, and outposts in the northern region. They also encouraged loyal families to move there. Soldiers were stationed to guard against raids, and deals were sometimes made with local tribes. Over time, roads were improved, allowing for the movement of troops and trade caravans. This began a long process of knitting the north more closely into Goryeo's domain.

3.3 Life in the Northern Frontier

The northern frontier was a harsh land, with cold winters and rugged mountains. Farmers grew grains like barley and millet in the short growing seasons. Some areas also supported livestock, such as cattle and horses. Many people hunted in forests for wild animals, which provided meat and furs.

Because of the rough climate, communities in the north had to be practical. Houses were often built with thicker walls or partially dug into the ground to protect against freezing temperatures. Local people collected firewood to stay warm, and they stored extra food for long winters.

Life was not only about survival, though. Frontier towns often bustled with traders selling salt, dried fish, cloth, and tools. Soldiers from the capital came with new ideas and news from the royal court. Local families celebrated festivals just like in the south, though they might adapt them to the northern setting. For example, harvest ceremonies had special importance, as a good harvest could mean the difference between a comfortable winter and a difficult one.

3.4 Dealing with the Khitan (Liao Dynasty)

One major threat Goryeo faced in the north came from the Khitan people, who established the Liao Dynasty. The Khitan were skilled horsemen and strong warriors, controlling vast territories in Manchuria and beyond. They also wished to expand their domain.

Early in the Goryeo period, tension led to several conflicts with the Khitan. Goryeo tried both diplomacy and warfare to protect its borders. In some years, Goryeo sent tribute gifts to Liao, while at other times, they built stronger forts and prepared armies. Major invasions by the Khitan occurred in the 10th and 11th centuries, testing Goryeo's resolve.

Yet, Goryeo managed to hold its ground. Famous generals, such as Gang Gam-chan, led Goryeo troops to victories in important battles, including one near the Yalu (Amnok) River. These successes boosted the pride of the people and showed that Goryeo would defend its northern lands with courage. Over time, a fragile peace took shape, with neither side able to fully conquer the other.

3.5 Shifts in Power and the Rise of the Jurchen

After the Khitan threat eased, the Jurchen peoples in Manchuria grew in strength. They would later form the Jin Dynasty, which replaced the Liao Dynasty. Just like the Khitan, the Jurchen were fierce fighters and experts at cavalry warfare. Goryeo again faced a choice: stand against them or find ways to cooperate.

Some Goryeo rulers tried to remain friendly with the Jurchen, offering trade deals or gifts. Others relied on forts and stationed troops in the north. The Jurchen themselves were not all united. Different tribal groups sometimes fought among themselves, which allowed Goryeo to form alliances with certain Jurchen leaders against others.

During this time, northern Goryeo towns continued to grow. They became meeting points for various peoples—Goryeo settlers, local tribes, Jurchen merchants, and traveling monks. Even though wars were common, cultural exchange still happened. Some Jurchen adopted parts of Goryeo culture, wearing Goryeo-style clothes or learning bits of the language. Goryeo also benefited from northern products like furs and ginseng, which were highly valued.

3.6 Buddhism's Influence on the North

Buddhism was the main religion of Goryeo. Monks traveled all around the kingdom to teach and help build temples. Even the kings supported this faith, seeing it as a way to unite the people. In the north, Buddhism brought new art, architecture, and customs.

Many temples were set up in frontier regions. They were not only spiritual centers but also places of learning. Monks and local people worked together to carve Buddha images in rocks or to construct wooden halls. Such projects helped tie the north to the rest of Goryeo culturally.

Buddhist rituals, such as praying for peace or a good harvest, often took on local flavors in the north. For instance, festivals might mix older shamanistic practices with Buddhist chanting. Monks also offered comfort during times of conflict by caring for the wounded and giving food to the poor. This kindness made Buddhism popular across class lines, whether people lived in the south or in the colder northern frontier.

3.7 Government and Administration

Goryeo had a structured government system, with a king at the top and various offices managing taxes, military matters, and ceremonies. In the north, local governors were appointed by the court. Some were loyal noble families from the capital, while others were local leaders who pledged loyalty to the king.

Land ownership was crucial. The government tried to control who owned what land, assigning fields to officials based on their rank. This system aimed to make sure loyal people stayed in charge of vital farmland. However, in frontier areas, this was harder to enforce because of raids and shifting populations. Sometimes local leaders simply managed land on their own.

Communication with the capital could be slow. Roads were rough, especially in winter. Couriers on horseback carried messages, but heavy snow and steep mountains often caused delays. As a result, northern governors had to make many decisions themselves. This led to more independence compared to those in regions closer to Gaegyeong.

3.8 Social Classes and Everyday Work

Like in the rest of Goryeo, the northern part had a clear social structure. At the top were the royal family and high-ranking nobles. Below them came lower nobles and local officials. Then there were commoners—farmers, artisans, and traders. At the bottom were slaves or serfs, who had almost no freedom.

In northern villages, many people worked as farmers or herders. Because farmland was more limited, livestock played a bigger role. Horses, in particular, were very important for trade and warfare. Some families specialized in raising and training horses for the royal court. Others became skilled hunters or fur traders.

Women helped in fields, tended animals, and handled household duties. They were also active in local markets, selling dairy products, vegetables, or handmade clothes. Children learned basic tasks early, helping with chores or gathering firewood. Older children often followed their parents' trades, continuing the family's way of life.

3.9 Trade Routes Through the North

While the capital and southern regions often focused on maritime trade with China or other countries, the north served as a land bridge. People traveling from Manchuria or beyond would pass through the northern parts of Goryeo, bringing goods such as animal skins, medicinal herbs, and metals.

Goryeo merchants sold rice, textiles, and pottery, among other items. Although the northern terrain was hard to cross, those who succeeded in trading could earn large profits. This made some frontier towns quite prosperous. Local inns appeared, offering food and shelter to traders. Blacksmiths and craft workers opened shops to sell tools, weapons, and simple household items.

With trade came cultural exchange. Foreign travelers brought news, stories, and new ideas about religion or technology. Monks who went on pilgrimages outside Goryeo might return with different styles of Buddhist art. Over time, these influences blended with local traditions, shaping the unique flavor of northern life.

3.10 Mongol Invasions and Their Impact

In the 13th century, a new threat emerged from the north: the Mongols. They built a huge empire across Asia, conquering many lands. At first, Goryeo tried diplomacy, sending envoys to meet Mongol leaders. However, disagreements arose, and the Mongols began to raid Goryeo.

The northern areas were the first to feel the brunt of these invasions. Mongol armies were fast and well-organized. They often seized small forts before Goryeo's main troops could react. People in frontier towns fled south, seeking safety. Crops were burned, and houses destroyed, causing fear and hardship.

Goryeo's royal court eventually decided to move the capital to Ganghwa Island, off the west coast, for protection. From there, they tried to fight back. But many northern regions remained under threat for years. After long and painful conflicts, Goryeo made a treaty with the Mongols. Although the kingdom survived, it had to accept Mongol control in many areas. The northern borders, in particular, felt the effects of Mongol oversight.

3.11 The Mongol Yuan Influence

Once Goryeo and the Mongols formed an uneasy peace, the Mongols set up the Yuan Dynasty in China. Goryeo became a kind of tributary state, meaning it had to pay tribute to the Yuan and follow certain rules. This arrangement deeply affected the north, since the Mongols had direct interests in border zones.

Some Mongols even settled in Goryeo, marrying into noble families. The royal court had Mongol princesses who married Goryeo kings. This led to mixed Goryeo-Mongol children, who often held high positions. The Mongols demanded resources such as horses and people to serve in labor or the military. Because the north was known for breeding horses, it faced heavier burdens.

Despite these hardships, cultural exchange also happened. New clothing styles, food, and customs arrived from the Mongol world. Some of these took root in the north, mixing with local ways. Over time, the Yuan Dynasty weakened, and Goryeo began to regain its independence. Yet, the period of Mongol control left a mark on northern society and politics.

3.12 Buddhism and Neo-Confucianism

By the late Goryeo era, another belief system started to gain strength: Neo-Confucianism. This was a form of Confucian thought that placed importance on moral behavior, social order, and proper governance. Some scholars in Goryeo believed that Neo-Confucianism would make the government more effective.

However, Buddhism was still strong, especially in northern monasteries that had fewer direct connections to the capital's new trends. Monks, donors, and local officials supported temple building and ceremonies. But in the royal court, the shift toward Neo-Confucian values began to influence policies. More officials promoted Confucian-based schools and exams, which eventually challenged Buddhism's power.

In the north, people sometimes found these new Confucian ideas confusing. They had grown up with Buddhism and older local traditions. Yet, government offices started to adopt Confucian rules for promotions and punishments. Over time, these ideas shaped how officials ran their towns, and younger generations studied Confucian ethics alongside Buddhist teachings.

3.13 Military Clashes and Rebellions

The late Goryeo period was also marked by internal struggles. Powerful generals or local leaders sometimes rebelled against the king or against other influential families. In the north, some groups felt neglected by the capital. They had suffered during the Mongol invasions and still faced raids from northern tribes.

Local uprisings happened when people were unhappy with heavy taxes, forced labor, or corruption among nobles. In some cases, rebels took over forts or threatened trade routes. The royal court had to send armies to restore order, or they appointed new governors who promised to address complaints.

At times, leaders of these rebellions used local pride to rally people. They reminded them of Goguryeo's mighty past or promised a better life if the north became independent. Most of these revolts were crushed, but they showed deep frustration that existed in certain frontier regions. These tensions would carry over when Goryeo eventually gave way to a new dynasty.

3.14 The End of Goryeo and Transition to Joseon

By the 14th century, Goryeo was declining. The royal court was divided, with some factions supporting Mongol interests and others wanting to push them out. Natural disasters and repeated conflicts further weakened the kingdom. Also, the spread of Neo-Confucian ideas made many officials doubt the policies of the old leadership.

A strong general named Yi Seong-gye rose to prominence. He gained fame defending the northern borders against invaders. When the royal court ordered him to attack the rising Ming Dynasty in China, he refused, believing it was a bad plan. Instead, he turned his troops around and took control of the government.

In 1392, Yi Seong-gye became the first king of the new Joseon Dynasty. Goryeo's rule ended, and a new era began. Though the capital moved south to Hanyang (Seoul), the north still remained an important zone. Joseon would continue to manage northern defenses, deal with tribes beyond the border, and keep building on the legacies left by Goryeo.

3.15 Legacy of the Goryeo Period in the North

The Goryeo Dynasty left a lasting impact on the north. People in these areas experienced many wars and shifting alliances. They also saw cultural blending, thanks to contact with the Khitan, Jurchen, Mongols, and others. Monasteries and temples in the north preserved Buddhist writings and art, some of which survived into later centuries.

During Goryeo, the north played a crucial part in the kingdom's defense. Many fortresses and watchtowers dotted the landscape. Roads connecting these outposts laid the groundwork for future development. Trade routes, though sometimes dangerous, brought prosperity to certain frontier towns.

At the same time, Goryeo's struggles with outside powers showed that controlling the north was never easy. The climate was rough, and neighboring peoples were often strong. Still, Goryeo leaders believed that the spirit of Goguryeo lived on in these lands, giving them a special pride and determination. This sense of a northern identity would continue into the Joseon era and beyond.

3.16 Summary and Reflection

The Goryeo Dynasty marks a key chapter in Korea's history, including the north's story. Founded by Wang Geon, Goryeo connected its new government to the memory of Goguryeo, aiming to recover and protect northern territories. Throughout its rule, Goryeo faced threats from the Khitan, Jurchen, and Mongols. Yet it also engaged in diplomacy, trade, and cultural exchange.

Buddhism flourished during this time, touching both the capital and outlying areas. Meanwhile, Neo-Confucianism started to gain ground, preparing the way for big changes. People in the north lived through invasions, forced labor, and occasional rebellions, but they also saw improvements in roads, temples, and markets. Goryeo eventually collapsed, but it left behind strong traditions. The north, shaped by Goryeo's achievements and troubles, would remain vital as a new dynasty took the stage.

CHAPTER 4

THE JOSEON DYNASTY'S INFLUENCE ON NORTHERN REGIONS

Introduction

The Joseon Dynasty began in 1392 and lasted until 1897. During these five centuries, Korea's rulers reshaped government, society, and culture in ways that still have an impact today. For the north, Joseon brought both continuity and change. Many of Goryeo's old structures remained, but Joseon leaders had their own plans. They embraced Neo-Confucianism as the guiding principle, restructuring the kingdom's laws, taxes, and daily life to fit Confucian ideals.

In this chapter, we will explore how the northern parts of Korea fit into Joseon's larger vision. We will see how the royal court tried to secure borders, manage trade, and oversee local affairs. We will also learn about how northern people lived during this period—how they farmed, how they prayed, and how they handled frequent threats from beyond the frontier. We will discuss cultural growth, including art, literature, and the influence of Confucian learning. Finally, we will look at major events and how they shaped the north as Joseon moved closer to more modern times.

4.1 Founding of the Joseon Dynasty

Yi Seong-gye, also known as King Taejo, was the founder of Joseon. Once a Goryeo general, he seized power and ended the old dynasty. He then chose Hanyang (modern-day Seoul) as the new capital, a location more central in the Korean Peninsula than Kaesong (Gaegyeong). This shift in capital signaled that Joseon wanted a fresh start.

Still, the new rulers could not ignore the north. Many of Yi Seong-gye's earlier battles had been fought along the northern borders. He knew those lands needed good administration to prevent rebellions and foreign invasions. Early in his reign, King Taejo and his advisors kept an eye on local power groups in the frontier, making sure they stayed loyal. Some rebellious leaders who refused to accept the new order were removed.

Joseon also benefited from the decline of the Mongol Yuan Dynasty. As Ming China rose, the balance of power in East Asia changed. Joseon recognized the Ming as the main regional power and formed a tributary relationship. This allowed Joseon to focus on its own internal matters, including the strengthening of northern defenses without constant Mongol threats.

4.2 Neo-Confucian Ideals and Their Effect on the North

From the start, Joseon's official ideology was Neo-Confucianism. King Taejo and his successors believed that a well-ordered society should follow Confucian values such as loyalty to the ruler, respect for elders, and proper conduct in all relationships. This system influenced every part of daily life, from government exams to family traditions.

In the north, Confucian schools, called hyanggyo, were built to educate local elites. Scholars from the capital traveled to these schools to teach the Confucian classics. Younger students learned about moral behavior, rituals, and history. Over time, many northern families sent their sons to study in these academies, hoping they could pass the government exams (gwageo) and become officials.

However, not everyone found it easy to adopt these new standards. Local customs, especially in more rural and mountainous areas, sometimes clashed with strict Confucian codes. Some people held onto folk traditions or Buddhist practices that had deep roots. The government tried to limit Buddhist influence, closing or reducing the size of many temples. Yet in the frontier, where the state's control was weaker, Buddhism stayed important, and shamanistic beliefs also remained strong.

4.3 Administrative Restructuring and Local Officials

Joseon divided the kingdom into provinces, each managed by a governor appointed by the king. Smaller administrative units, like counties and prefectures, were also created. This clear system made it easier for the central government to collect taxes, manage soldiers, and enforce laws. The northern areas were included in these divisions, though they sometimes had extra steps for defense because of border concerns.

Local officials often faced unique challenges in the north. Harsh weather made travel difficult. Trade routes were long and could be unsafe. Many villagers lived far apart, in secluded valleys or along riverbanks near mountains. Gaining their trust was not always easy, especially if officials appeared more interested in tax collection than in helping solve local problems.

Still, some officials earned respect by building roads, digging irrigation canals, or setting up markets. They also played a role in settling conflicts between families or clans. Local offices became centers where disputes could be heard, and punishments or fines were decided. Over time, a mix of local customs and central regulations emerged, giving the north a degree of stability under Joseon rule.

4.4 Securing the Borders Against Jurchen and Other Groups

Even though the Mongol threat faded, new problems arose with the Jurchen tribes. Some Jurchen groups still lived in Manchuria and along the northern frontier of Joseon. They would sometimes raid border towns, stealing livestock or capturing people. Joseon responded by building fortresses, watchtowers, and walls at key points. Soldiers were stationed in garrisons, and local militias were organized to help in emergencies.

Joseon leaders also tried to use diplomacy. They traded with certain Jurchen chiefs, giving them gifts and goods in exchange for loyalty or peace treaties. This strategy worked at times, but not always. The Jurchen themselves were not united, and some groups ignored these deals.

As decades passed, one Jurchen group rose in power: the Later Jin, which eventually became the Qing Dynasty in China. Joseon would later face serious conflicts with them, but for now, the main goal was simply to keep border regions safe. The north remained an active frontier, with watchful soldiers and local people ready to defend their land if needed.

4.5 Farming and Land Use in the Northern Regions

Joseon placed great importance on agriculture. Taxes on crops supported the royal court, the military, and public works. In the north, farmland was less plentiful due to cold weather and rugged terrain. Still, the government encouraged settlers to move north, promising them land to farm.

These settlers faced many hardships. Clearing forests or mountain slopes to create fields was tough work. The growing season was short, and harsh winters could kill crops or livestock. But some settlers persevered, using hardy grains like barley or millet. Over time, small farming communities grew, building shared irrigation systems when possible.

In addition to crops, animal husbandry remained important. The north was famous for producing good horses, which the royal court and military needed. Cattle and sheep also thrived in certain areas. By raising livestock, northern farmers could trade meat, hides, or wool with southern merchants for rice, salt, and other goods. This helped them survive even if their harvests were poor.

4.6 The Role of Trade and Markets

Trade within Joseon was vital to connect the north with the rest of the kingdom. Mountain passes often slowed travel, so the government built roads and posted stations where travelers could rest. Markets sprang up along these routes. Local farmers and herders sold their produce, while merchants from the south brought textiles, pottery, and books.

Some larger towns in the north became administrative centers, hosting regular market days. People would gather to barter goods, exchange news, and form business ties. Officials sometimes oversaw these markets to ensure fair prices and keep out thieves. Trade also involved some border transactions with Jurchen or Chinese merchants, although these were carefully watched.

Over time, wealthier families in the north emerged, often thanks to successful trade ventures. They might deal in animal products like furs or leather. Others specialized in medicinal herbs collected in the mountains. These families, though not as grand as noble clans in the capital, gained local influence. Some married into lower-level noble families or sent their sons to study in Confucian schools, hoping to rise further in society.

4.7 Confucian Ethics and Social Life

In Joseon, Confucian principles shaped family and social life. The father was the head of the household, and respect for elders was key. Ancestral rites, where families honored their ancestors with simple offerings, became common. People in the north, even those living in isolated villages, tried to follow these practices.

Marriages were arranged through family negotiations, and brides often moved to live with the groom's family. Women's roles were mostly tied to home and family, though in frontier areas, they sometimes worked in fields or ran small market stalls. Education for girls was less formal, but they could learn basic reading or needlework at home.

Villagers held local festivals, often tied to the agricultural cycle. They might celebrate planting time in spring or give thanks after harvest in autumn. These events mixed Confucian rituals with older shamanistic customs. For example, a village might hold a Confucian-style ceremony for the harvest, but also invite a shaman to perform dances or prayers for a bountiful next year. This blending was common in the north, where old beliefs stayed strong.

4.8 Military Defense and the Four Garrisons

During the 15th and 16th centuries, the Joseon royal court set up a system known as the Four Garrisons in the northern region. These were key fortress towns, each guarding strategic points along the frontier. Soldiers stationed there served as the first line of defense against raids or invasions.

The soldiers had several duties. They patrolled the borders, built watchtowers, and trained local militias. They also helped settle new villages, protecting farmers who moved north. The government provided some land to the soldiers so they could grow food for themselves and avoid being a heavy burden on the local population.

Sometimes, these garrisons cooperated with friendly Jurchen groups to keep the peace. But if fighting broke out with hostile tribes, the garrisons were expected to hold off attacks until reinforcements arrived from the capital. Over time, this system helped stabilize the frontier, though it never completely removed the risk of conflict.

4.9 Japanese and Other External Threats

The Imjin War (1592–1598) was a major event in Joseon history when Japanese forces invaded Korea. Although the main battles took place in the south and around the capital, the north also felt the impact. Soldiers and resources were pulled from the frontier to fight in central areas, leaving some northern towns more vulnerable to raids from across the border.

After the war ended, Joseon was weakened. This allowed the Jurchen (who would soon be called the Manchu or Qing) to grow even stronger. In the early 17th century, the Manchu launched invasions of Joseon, again testing the kingdom's defenses. Many northern villages suffered looting, and people fled south in fear.

Though these invasions ended with Joseon paying tribute to the Manchu, the kingdom realized it needed to further improve its military. Officials studied new defense strategies, including better fortress designs. The north, already familiar with conflict, now became a critical focus of the kingdom's security planning, as the Manchu territory was directly across the border.

4.10 Cultural and Intellectual Growth

Joseon was well-known for its achievements in literature, art, and science. The creation of Hangul by King Sejong in the 15th century allowed more people to read and write in Korean. Even in the north, some scholars used Hangul for local writings and record-keeping. Though many officials still valued classical Chinese for official documents, Hangul slowly spread among common people.

Scholarship in Confucian philosophy flourished, with various academies (seowon) popping up in different provinces. Northern families who gained wealth sometimes funded these academies, hoping to raise the status of their region. Students there studied Confucian classics, wrote poetry, and debated ethical issues.

Artists also drew inspiration from the northern landscape. Paintings of mountains, rivers, and winter scenes became popular themes. While most famous artists lived near the capital, some traveled north to capture the region's rugged beauty. Over time, poems and stories about frontier life appeared, sharing tales of brave soldiers, wise officials, and everyday villagers facing nature's challenges.

4.11 Religious Practices and Folk Beliefs

Neo-Confucianism dominated the royal court, yet in the north, Buddhism, shamanism, and folk customs remained strong. Temples in remote mountain areas kept old rituals alive. Monks sometimes provided free medicine, shelter, or basic education, earning local gratitude.

Shamans, often women, performed ceremonies to appease spirits, cure illnesses, or ensure good harvests. Even some officials secretly consulted shamans, despite Confucian rules against such "superstitions." Folk festivals often mixed Confucian, Buddhist, and shamanic elements, creating a unique blend of traditions.

Ancestor worship was a key part of Confucian belief. Families maintained small ancestral shrines and held memorial rites on special days. In the north, these rites might also include offerings to mountain or river spirits, reflecting older local practices. Such customs show how people adapted official teachings to their real-life environments, especially in frontier regions where nature was both a friend and a foe.

4.12 Local Rebellions and Unrest

Throughout Joseon, there were times when commoners rose up against heavy taxes, forced labor, or corrupt officials. The north, with its frequent hardships, was not immune to such unrest. When harvests failed or soldiers demanded more supplies, villagers sometimes resisted.

Some rebels took refuge in the mountains, forming small bands that attacked wealthy estates or government offices. They saw themselves as protectors of the poor, punishing greedy officials or landlords. The royal court dispatched troops to quell these uprisings and restore order. In some cases, rebellious leaders claimed to follow an old prophecy about a new age of fairness, hoping to win local support.

Most rebellions did not last long, but they showed that life in the north could be harsh and that people would protest if they felt pushed too far.

Joseon kings often tried to respond with a mix of force and reforms. They might reduce taxes, send relief grain to starving villages, or punish corrupt officials. However, the underlying problems—limited farmland, cold climates, and distance from the capital—remained hard to solve.

4.13 The Manchu (Qing) Invasions and Northern Hardships

As mentioned before, the Manchu invasions of the early 17th century severely tested Joseon's northern defenses. The first invasion in 1627 and the second in 1636 both led to great suffering. Northern towns were raided, and many people were taken captive or killed. Even the royal family had to flee to a fortress in the south during the second invasion.

After these invasions, Joseon entered into a tributary relationship with the Qing Dynasty. While this meant peace, it also confirmed that Joseon had to respect the Qing as its suzerain. The border areas again saw changes, as Manchu forces sometimes patrolled near the boundary, and trade with the Qing grew.

For common people in the north, rebuilding took time. Farms and villages damaged in the invasions needed new settlers or returning refugees. The government offered tax breaks to encourage resettlement. Slowly, life returned to normal, though many families never fully recovered from the violence or loss of relatives to Manchu captivity.

4.14 Positive Exchanges with the Qing

Despite the painful invasions, relations between Joseon and the Qing did not stay entirely hostile. Over the years, merchants, scholars, and diplomats traveled between the two states. The Qing capital (in what is now Beijing) became a place where Joseon diplomats learned about new books, technologies, and cultural ideas.

Some northern border towns turned into trading hubs, where Qing merchants and Korean traders exchanged goods. Furs, ginseng, and medicinal herbs were common exports from the Korean side. Meanwhile, items like silk, advanced weapons, or unique foods came from the Qing. This commerce helped northern areas recover and gain some wealth.

Scholars who visited Qing territory brought back knowledge about Western science and other foreign ideas that were reaching China. Although Joseon remained quite closed to the outside world, small bits of global information trickled in through these channels. Northern officials who dealt with border management sometimes knew more about these international currents than their southern counterparts.

4.15 The 18th and 19th Centuries: Shifts and Struggles

During the 18th century, some Joseon kings like Yeongjo and Jeongjo tried new reforms. They wanted to improve the kingdom's systems, reduce corruption, and help common people. However, these measures often centered on the capital and southern provinces. Northern regions got fewer benefits due to their distance and rugged conditions.

The 19th century brought more challenges. Floods, droughts, and famines struck the country. The government, strained by internal power struggles, sometimes failed to provide relief. Northern provinces, already less fertile, suffered heavily. People faced hunger, and some traveled south or to China to find food or work.

Foreign ships and ideas also began appearing near Korea's coasts, pushing the kingdom toward eventual contact with Western nations. Yet, these influences mostly affected the south first. The north, though not untouched, remained a bit more isolated. However, rumors of foreigners and new religions, like Catholicism, reached even remote villages, causing curiosity and worry.

4.16 Social Transformations in the Late Joseon North

During the later Joseon era, social lines started to blur a bit. Some noble families (yangban) lost wealth, while certain commoner or merchant families gained it. This happened in the north too. Successful merchants might buy land, dress more finely, and even arrange good marriages for their children, hoping to climb the social ladder.

Education played a key role. Although the top government posts still required passing the Confucian civil service exams, new ideas about commerce and regional development emerged. Some local elites promoted better farming methods or created private academies. They sought to improve life in their region instead of relying on the capital.

Still, strict hierarchies remained. Slavery persisted, though it gradually declined in the 19th century. Women stayed mostly in domestic roles, with few chances for formal schooling. The mix of slow progress and deep-rooted traditions defined the north's society in the final century of Joseon rule.

4.17 The Northern Regions on the Eve of Modern Changes

By the late 19th century, Joseon faced growing pressure from foreign powers. Japan, Russia, and Western countries all showed interest in the peninsula's strategic location. The north, sharing borders with China and having access to seas close to Russia, became an area of special focus.

Joseon's royal court, divided and struggling with internal reform debates, tried to maintain old ways while also adopting some modern measures. In the north, a few new roads or telegraph lines appeared. Foreign missionaries and traders sometimes traveled there, bringing new beliefs, products, or medicine. Local reaction was mixed—some welcomed the potential benefits, while others feared outside control.

During this period, people in the north still remembered Goryeo and Goguryeo's legacies. They had lived for centuries in an environment of shifting power and constant adaptation. This sense of a unique northern identity would carry into the modern era, although this book does not focus on those more recent times.

4.18 Conclusion

The Joseon Dynasty deeply shaped the north of the Korean Peninsula. It established lasting administrative systems, spread Confucian ideals, and worked to secure its frontiers from repeated threats. Over five centuries, northern communities balanced official rules with their own local customs, including older Buddhist and shamanistic practices. They endured invasions, natural disasters, and social inequalities but also found ways to trade, farm, and preserve a rich cultural life.

From the founding by Yi Seong-gye to the later periods of struggle and limited reform, the north played a critical role in Joseon's story. It was both a borderland and a place where Korea's diverse heritage thrived. As Joseon neared the dawn of modern times, the north remained full of potential and challenges alike. In the next chapters, we will continue our journey through the history that leads up to the creation and evolution of what we know today as North Korea, focusing on more events but still staying within historical frames, so we can see how these roots grew and changed over time.

CHAPTER 5

FOREIGN INVASIONS AND CHANGES IN POWER

Introduction

By the time we reach the middle and later parts of the Joseon Dynasty, the Korean Peninsula had seen many forms of conflict. From the early power struggles to the strong influence of Confucian values, Joseon rulers worked hard to protect their land and maintain order. Still, foreign threats often tested their strength. In this chapter, we will look at major invasions that happened during Joseon, how these wars changed the kingdom's power structure, and what it meant for the people—especially those in the north.

We will begin with the Japanese invasions of the late 16th century, often called the Imjin War. These invasions shook Joseon to its core. Next, we will explore the Manchu invasions that followed in the 17th century, which brought new challenges from the north. We will see how these events forced Joseon's rulers to rethink policies, military organization, and diplomacy. We will also discuss how the northern regions, already on the frontier, faced unique struggles during these times of foreign intrusion.

5.1 Background: Joseon Before the Storm

Before the big invasions, Joseon had been relatively stable under kings like Sejong (the creator of Hangul) and Sejo. Confucian ideals guided government and education. Farming was the backbone of the economy, and the capital in Hanyang (Seoul) grew in culture and population. Scholars debated how best to run the kingdom, focusing on moral values and the welfare of the people.

Yet, troubles lurked beneath the surface. The military was sometimes neglected because the kingdom had enjoyed a long period of peace. Officials in the court argued over how much attention or funding the army needed. Some believed that focusing on culture and Confucian learning was more important than spending large sums on defense. This left Joseon less prepared for the storms that were about to hit.

In the north, life went on with farming, herding, and frontier trade. People there relied on watchtowers and small garrisons for safety, expecting occasional border raids rather than full-scale invasions. No one anticipated that large armies might arrive from other directions with the aim of conquering the whole peninsula.

5.2 The Imjin War: Japanese Invasions (1592–1598)

In 1592, Japan, led by the warlord Toyotomi Hideyoshi, launched a massive invasion of Joseon. Their aim was to march quickly through Korea and use it as a path to attack China. The sudden assault caught Joseon unprepared. Japanese troops landed in the south and moved rapidly northward, capturing key cities and towns.

1. **Early Japanese Victories**
   - The Japanese brought modern firearms, especially muskets, which gave them an advantage.
   - Joseon's royal court panicked, and the king fled north for safety.
   - Many local officials abandoned their posts, causing confusion among the people.

2. **Joseon's Fight Back**
   - Admiral Yi Sun-sin led the navy to important victories at sea, thanks to strong warships called "turtle ships."
   - Guerrilla forces, known as **righteous armies**, formed among commoners and local leaders. They attacked Japanese soldiers in smaller raids.
   - Ming China sent aid to Joseon, leading to combined Joseon-Ming forces.

The war dragged on for years, with a second invasion in 1597. Although the Japanese held some ground, they met fierce resistance. Hideyoshi died in 1598, and Japan withdrew, ending the invasions.

5.3 Impact of the Imjin War on Northern Regions

While the heaviest fighting happened in the south and central areas, the north also felt the effects of the Imjin War:

- **Resource Drain**: Troops and supplies were pulled from the northern frontiers to fight the Japanese in southern and central fronts. This left border outposts weaker against local raids.
- **Refugees**: Civilians fleeing battles in the south sometimes traveled all the way north, seeking safer places. This caused overcrowding in some towns, where food was already limited.
- **Disruption of Trade**: Merchants who carried goods from the south to the north faced blocked roads and danger from roaming bandits. Trade routes became unsafe, harming local markets in the north.

In the aftermath, Joseon's entire society had to rebuild. Cities were in ruins, farmland was damaged, and the population had dropped. The government realized it had to reform the military, fortify defenses, and pay closer attention to border security.

5.4 Post-War Reforms and Power Shifts

The Imjin War showed Joseon's weaknesses. In response, the court introduced changes:

1. **Military Improvements**
    - Upgrading fortresses, especially in strategic areas like the northern borders.
    - Training and equipping troops more effectively, with better discipline and newer firearms.
    - Creating a more structured system for calling peasants to military service when needed.

2. **Government Restructuring**
    - Officials who had abandoned their duties or performed poorly were sometimes punished.

- Some reforms tried to limit corruption in local offices.
 - More attention was paid to tax collection fairness, so peasants did not bear all the burdens.

3. **Rise of Military Leaders**

    - The war turned generals and admirals into heroes. Figures like Admiral Yi Sun-sin were praised and honored for their defense of the nation.
    - However, in the day-to-day court politics, civil officials still held the highest power. The Confucian scholar-official class (yangban) remained influential, often pushing military leaders aside once the war ended.

These efforts aimed to prepare Joseon for future threats. Yet, the kingdom was financially drained. Farmland had to be restored, and many roads and bridges needed repairs. This was a slow process, leaving the kingdom vulnerable to the next big challenge—this time from the north.

5.5 The Rise of the Manchu Threat

Meanwhile, in the region north of Korea, the Jurchen tribes were growing stronger under a new leader, Nurhaci. He united various Jurchen clans and formed a state that would later become the Qing Dynasty. At first, the Jurchen had some peaceful ties with Joseon, trading goods across the border. But as the Jurchen grew more powerful, they looked to expand.

Joseon's leaders were uncertain how to handle this new neighbor. Some officials wanted to stay on friendly terms, giving gifts or paying tribute. Others argued that Joseon should ally with the Ming Dynasty in China against the rising Jurchen power. This split caused tension in the royal court.

Moreover, Joseon was still recovering from the Imjin War. Parts of the north were not fully rebuilt, and many local garrisons lacked supplies. The kingdom's leaders tried to fortify key points, but they did not expect a large-scale invasion so soon.

5.6 The First Manchu Invasion (1627)

In 1627, the Manchu (led by Nurhaci's son and successor, Hong Taiji) launched their first major invasion of Joseon:

1. **Sudden Attack**

    - Manchu forces crossed the Yalu (Amnok) River quickly.
    - Northern forts fell or surrendered, with some local officials unsure of how to respond.
    - Many northern villagers fled south, remembering the horrors of the previous war.

2. **Joseon's Response**

    - King Injo and his court retreated to Ganghwa Island, off the west coast, much like the royal family had done during the Mongol invasions centuries earlier.
    - Some generals tried to organize a defense, but the Manchu cavalry was swift and well-trained.

The Manchu demanded Joseon end its ties with the Ming and pay tribute to them instead. The war ended in a peace deal where Joseon agreed to sign a treaty. Although the kingdom remained independent, it had to acknowledge the Manchu as a more powerful neighbor.

5.7 The Second Manchu Invasion (1636)

Peace did not last long. Tensions rose again when King Injo secretly sent messages of loyalty to the Ming. Angered by this betrayal, the Manchu returned:

1. **Seoul Captured**

    - Manchu troops bypassed many forts and marched toward the capital.
    - King Injo tried to hide in Namhansanseong, a mountain fortress near the capital, but the Manchu surrounded it.

2. **Surrender**

    - After a long siege, King Injo surrendered in early 1637.
    - He had to perform a humiliating ritual, bowing to the Manchu leader to show obedience.
    - Many nobles wept at this event, seeing it as a great shame for Joseon.

From this point on, Joseon became a "tributary state" of the Manchu, who soon established the Qing Dynasty in China. Joseon was forced to pay tribute and send hostages, often young princes or noble children, to the Qing court as a show of loyalty.

5.8 Effects of the Manchu Invasions on the North

Because the invasions came from the north, northern regions experienced heavy fighting and major disruption:

- **Destroyed Settlements**: Manchu troops sometimes burned villages, took food, and captured people.
- **Forced Loyalty**: After the wars, the Manchu demanded that local leaders pledge loyalty to the Qing. Some local officials adapted to this new order, while others resisted.
- **Border Management**: Joseon strengthened border fortresses even more after the second invasion, trying to prevent future attacks. Soldiers were stationed in small groups, always on guard.

These invasions caused tremendous sorrow and anger throughout Joseon. Many people blamed the royal court for poor decisions. The memory of King Injo's surrender lived on as a national shame, influencing how future kings dealt with foreign powers.

5.9 Changes in Power and Policy After the Wars

Following these painful wars, Joseon had to adjust:

1. **Tributary Ties to the Qing**

    - Joseon regularly sent missions to the Qing court with gifts.

    - This relationship ensured peace for many years, though Joseon had to remain cautious about its northern neighbor.

2. **Rise of a "Small China" Idea**

    - After the Manchu conquered the Ming and established the Qing Dynasty in China, many Joseon scholars refused to accept the Qing as the rightful heirs of Chinese civilization.

    - They promoted the idea that Joseon should uphold Confucian values and see itself as the last true guardian of Ming culture.

    - This mindset influenced art, clothing styles, and the official view of the north. The frontier once again became a place of defense against "barbarian" influence.

3. **Military Rebuilding**

    - The kingdom tried to keep a stronger standing army, though budget issues and internal politics made this hard.

- More fortresses were upgraded, and watchtowers were built along key river crossings.

4. **Social Shifts**

    - Many families lost members who were taken as captives to the Qing lands.

    - This led to grief and a deep sense of longing for revenge or, at least, redemption.

    - Some captives eventually returned with stories of life in the Qing Empire, adding new cultural influences to Joseon society.

5.10 Internal Power Struggles in Joseon

Even as Joseon adjusted to life under Qing influence, internal power struggles grew. Various factions at the royal court fought for control. Civil officials (the yangban class) often split into different groups, each claiming to be the true guardian of Confucian values.

1. **Factions (Parties) at Court**

    - The main factions included the Westerners, Southerners, Northerners, and Easterners, though they often changed names and alliances.

    - They argued over policies, appointments to official posts, and foreign relations.

2. **Impact on Northern Governance**

    - When one faction won power, it might replace governors in northern provinces with its own allies.

    - These constant changes made local governance less stable.

    - The north needed steady leadership to recover from invasions, but instead, it got shifting policies from whichever faction held power in the capital.

3. **Corruption and Neglect**

    - Some local officials used their posts to enrich themselves. They collected heavy taxes from farmers and kept much of the wealth.

    - People in the north felt the court was not paying attention to their needs. This tension would later lead to unrest and peasant uprisings.

5.11 Impact on Common People

For ordinary villagers, foreign invasions and power struggles meant:

- **Heavy Tax Burdens**: Wars cost money, so the government raised taxes or demanded labor from farmers to rebuild defenses and roads.
- **Hard Lives**: Fields were often ruined by marching troops, making it hard to grow enough food.
- **Displacement**: Families who lost their homes sometimes never returned. Some wandered south or even crossed into Qing territory looking for work.
- **Cultural Anxiety**: Stories of invasions made people fearful of strangers. Northern communities were extra watchful, keeping weapons at home in case of raids.

At the same time, life had to go on. Villagers rebuilt houses, re-dug irrigation ditches, and tried to put the wars behind them. Local markets slowly reopened, and trade routes were cleared. Over decades, the scars began to heal, though the memory of those invasions lasted for generations.

5.12 Rebounding Economy and Growing Culture

Despite the hardships, Joseon entered a period of relative peace under Qing rule. The court began to focus again on economic and cultural growth:

1. **Agricultural Improvements**

    - More farmland was reclaimed or newly developed in the north.
    - Crop rotation and better tools helped increase harvests.
    - Some peasants moved to less populated northern areas, hoping to find land of their own.

2. **Arts and Scholarship**

    - Neo-Confucian studies flourished again, with new academies popping up even in remote provinces.

- Painting, pottery, and literature saw renewed attention. Some works depicted the harsh times of war, while others praised the peaceful countryside.
- Scholars wrote about the north's landscapes, including mountains and rivers, which began to appear more often in art and poetry.

3. **Trade with the Qing**

- After the invasions, official relations with the Qing allowed for controlled trade.
- Northern border towns became markets for exchanging goods like ginseng, furs, and grains.
- Some merchants made considerable profits, boosting local wealth.

Still, under the surface, tensions remained. Many Koreans felt humiliated by the past wars and the tribute system. There was also worry that the royal court, caught up in factional rivalries, might neglect the welfare of the provinces again if a new threat emerged.

5.13 Ongoing Threat of Raids

Even though large-scale invasions eased, smaller raids never stopped completely. Bandits or rogue groups from beyond the northern border would sneak across to steal horses or livestock. Forts near the frontier had to stay alert, rotating watch duty day and night.

Local militias formed, where villagers trained occasionally with bows or spears. Older men taught younger ones how to recognize warning signals from watchtowers. A system of beacon fires on hilltops allowed them to quickly spread the alarm if they saw strange troops coming. This network had existed in earlier times but was improved after learning painful lessons from the Imjin War and the Manchu invasions.

5.14 Social Changes Among the Northern Populations

One key development after the invasions was the gradual mix of different groups in the north:

- **Returned Captives**: Some Koreans who had been taken to Qing lands managed to come back years later. They brought new habits, clothing styles, or even tastes in food. This exposure to outside customs made certain villages quite diverse.
- **Refugees from the South**: People who had lost everything in the war sometimes moved north, attracted by available land. They mingled with local families, forming new communities.
- **Shared Hardships**: Because everyone had suffered during invasions, there was a sense of unity among villagers, no matter their background. They worked together to rebuild roads, houses, and barns.

Despite the mixing of populations, the class system still held firm, with yangban at the top and commoners below them. But in the frontier, class rules could be slightly more relaxed, because survival and cooperation often mattered more than strict social rank.

5.15 Rise of Practical Learning (Silhak)

After seeing the devastation caused by war and the slow pace of rebuilding, some Joseon scholars proposed new ways of thinking. This movement was called **Silhak**, or "Practical Learning." Silhak scholars believed:

1. **Focus on Real Issues**: Instead of only studying ancient Confucian texts, they wanted to solve real problems, like improving farming techniques or building better irrigation.
2. **Fair Tax and Land Systems**: They argued that the tax system needed to be more equal, so the poor did not suffer while corrupt officials grew rich.
3. **Local Development**: They suggested studying local conditions, like soil quality or climate in northern regions, to help farmers grow more food.

While many powerful officials ignored or even punished Silhak scholars, their ideas slowly spread. In the north, some local leaders tried small-scale experiments, such as new farming methods. Over time, these approaches helped certain areas recover more quickly from war losses.

5.16 Diplomatic Shifts in East Asia

As the Qing Dynasty in China settled into power, the political map changed:

- **Stable Qing Rule**: The Qing ruled a vast empire. Many nations, including Joseon, kept tributary ties to avoid conflicts.
- **Decreased Threat from Japan**: After the Imjin War, Japan turned inward for a while. There were no more large invasions from that direction, though smaller incidents at sea sometimes happened.
- **Joseon's Position**: Joseon found a sort of balance, paying tribute to the Qing but also maintaining its own government. In effect, the kingdom's biggest external pressure point remained the northern border, where official trade and occasional smuggling mingled.

During this time, Joseon had room to rebuild its cities and culture. The capital thrived again, and the royal court funded various projects like palace expansions and a detailed nationwide land survey. However, the seeds of future turmoil were being planted by ongoing factional fights, social inequalities, and the memory of past humiliations.

5.17 Lasting Effects on Joseon Society

The foreign invasions of the late 16th and early 17th centuries had a deep impact:

1. **Military Awareness**: Even though peace followed, Joseon leaders never forgot how quickly an enemy could strike. This led to improved forts and defenses across the land.
2. **Diplomatic Caution**: The kingdom became more careful about foreign relations. Treaties and tribute missions were taken seriously to avoid provoking powerful neighbors.
3. **Cultural Pride and Isolation**: Many Koreans felt a renewed sense of identity. They wanted to preserve their customs and remain wary of outside influences.
4. **Economic Shifts**: War damage had forced some families to start fresh, sometimes leading to new opportunities or changes in social standing, though the class system still stood firm.

As Joseon moved into the later centuries, it carried both the scars of these invasions and the lessons learned. The kingdom would stay in this careful state until new challenges arose in the 19th century.

CHAPTER 6

THE LATE JOSEON PERIOD AND SHIFTS IN SOCIETY

Introduction

The Late Joseon Period, often considered the 18th and 19th centuries, brought a mix of challenges and growth to the Korean Peninsula. The kingdom tried to heal from earlier invasions and set up more stable governance. Some kings promoted reforms and cultural advances, yet major problems remained. Heavy taxes, corruption, natural disasters, and power struggles made life hard for ordinary people.

In this chapter, we will look at how Joseon society changed over these two centuries—especially in the north. We will explore new ideas in farming, education, and administration. We will see how some rulers tried to help the poor, while others focused on upholding Confucian traditions in strict ways. We will also discuss local uprisings and the continued influence of outside forces. By understanding these shifts, we get a clearer picture of the pressures that eventually led Korea toward the modern era.

6.1 Kings Yeongjo and Jeongjo: Era of Reform and Stability

Two prominent kings, Yeongjo (r. 1724–1776) and his grandson Jeongjo (r. 1776–1800), worked hard to strengthen the kingdom:

1. **Tax Reforms**

    - King Yeongjo introduced policies to reduce the tax burden on peasants. One well-known policy was the "Equalized Tax System," aiming to make taxes more fair.

    - Corrupt local officials were punished more often, at least in theory, improving life for many farmers.

2. **Encouraging Scholarship**

    - Both kings valued education. They supported scholars and built libraries.
    - Jeongjo founded the Gyujanggak library at the palace, which collected books and documents from around the kingdom.
    - These initiatives helped preserve and study works on history, Confucian philosophy, and science.

3. **Northern Involvement**

    - These reforms also reached northern provinces. More officials were dispatched to collect information on local needs.
    - Some roads were improved, helping traders travel between the north and the capital.
    - Confucian schools got better funding, allowing more local students to study, though access was still limited to certain social classes.

Kings Yeongjo and Jeongjo are remembered as leaders who tried to balance old Confucian ideals with practical governance. They cracked down on factional rivalries in the court, though such rivalries did not completely disappear. Their reigns saw relative peace and modest improvements in the standard of living for some people, including those in the north.

6.2 The Growth of Agriculture and Trade

During the 18th century, several factors boosted agriculture in Joseon:

- **Better Tools**: Iron plows and stronger hoes became more common, helping farmers cultivate land faster.
- **New Crops**: Some crops, like chili peppers and sweet potatoes, arrived through trade or foreign contact. They grew well in different soils and climates, giving farmers more options for food.
- **Irrigation Projects**: Small dams and canals were built in certain regions. Where these were successful, harvests improved greatly.

In the north, some farmers experimented with more hardy grain varieties, suitable for cold or mountainous terrain. Improved roads also allowed local goods—like furs, ginseng, and lumber—to reach markets in the capital. Some northern merchants formed trade networks, sending caravans south and sometimes even dealing with merchants from Qing China.

Still, farming in the north remained risky. Winters were long, and farmland was limited in many areas. If floods or droughts hit, it was difficult to recover. People often relied on livestock or hunting to supplement their diet, keeping the mixed economy of farming, herding, and trade alive.

6.3 Social Classes and Shifting Boundaries

Joseon society was traditionally divided into clear classes:

1. **Yangban (Nobles)**: These were scholar-officials or aristocrats. They lived in better homes, studied Confucian texts, and held government posts.
2. **Chungin (Middle Class)**: This included technical experts, translators, and minor officials.
3. **Sangmin (Commoners)**: Farmers, craftsmen, merchants, who made up most of the population.
4. **Cheonmin (Low-Born)**: Slaves, butchers, and other groups with low social status.

In the Late Joseon Period, these class boundaries began to blur a bit. Some merchant families became quite wealthy, sometimes rivaling poorer yangban families. A few commoners managed to buy official titles or bribe local officials for better status. This was more common in commercial hubs, including some northern trade towns.

At the same time, many yangban families in remote areas struggled financially. Even if they kept their noble status, they might have lost their land or money, making life difficult. This gap between official status and actual wealth caused social tension. People started to question whether the old system was fair or fit for changing times.

6.4 Confucian Ethics vs. Folk Beliefs

Confucianism remained the official teaching. Royal ceremonies, local governance, and family rituals all followed Confucian guidelines. But folk beliefs, including shamanism and Buddhism, still held strong in many areas:

- **Shamanistic Practices**: In the north, shamans (often women) performed rituals for healing, good harvests, or protection against evil spirits. Villagers turned to them during crises like famines or epidemics.
- **Buddhist Temples**: While Joseon's court favored Confucianism, some mountain temples in the north continued to serve local communities. Monks provided medicine or basic lessons, and commoners supported temples through donations.
- **Mixing Traditions**: Many families practiced Confucian ancestor rites but also visited a shaman for help with illnesses or consulted Buddhist monks before a long journey. This blending showed that everyday life did not neatly follow official rules.

These diverse spiritual practices helped people cope with the hardships of frontier life. They also showed how local culture could adapt, merging old beliefs with new philosophies.

6.5 The Silhak Movement (Practical Learning) Continues

Silhak, or Practical Learning, continued to gain followers in the 18th century. Silhak scholars looked for real solutions to common problems:

1. **Land Reform**: Some called for redistributing land so peasants would have enough to farm, reducing poverty.
2. **Agricultural Study**: Scholars researched better ways to grow crops, store grains, and manage irrigation.
3. **Geographical Surveys**: They mapped provinces more accurately, including the north's mountains and rivers, hoping to improve travel and find new farmland.

Despite these forward-thinking ideas, many officials in the capital resisted major changes. They worried that shaking up the land system might cause unrest among the powerful yangban class. Still, a few local administrators in the north tried small-scale experiments—like rotating crops or allowing peasants more freedom to sell their harvest.

6.6 Peasant Life and Local Markets

For most people in the north, daily life revolved around basic survival. Peasants focused on planting, harvesting, and raising livestock. When not in the fields, they repaired fences, stored firewood, or made simple clothing. Families helped one another, sharing tools or labor.

Local markets usually took place on a set schedule—every five days, for instance. These markets allowed villagers to trade:

- **Farm Produce**: Grains, vegetables, herbs.
- **Handicrafts**: Pots, wooden bowls, simple fabrics.
- **Livestock**: Chickens, pigs, or goats, sometimes sold or traded for other goods.

At these markets, peasants got news from traveling merchants or from neighbors who visited bigger towns. They learned about royal decrees or events in the capital. This information sharing was important in a time without modern media.

6.7 Northern Frontier Challenges

Frontier life remained tough. The mountainous north, especially near the Yalu (Amnok) and Tumen rivers, was distant from direct royal supervision. People lived in scattered villages or towns with small fortifications. The state kept some garrisons active, but they were not always well supplied.

Bandits sometimes roamed these borderlands. Locals had to be cautious when traveling, especially at night. Winter temperatures could be extreme, forcing families to stockpile food and firewood. Disease outbreaks were common, made worse by the difficulty of finding doctors or medicine.

On the other hand, some frontier areas prospered because of trade with Manchuria. Hunters sold furs and ginseng, while merchants from Qing lands traded fabrics, herbs, and sometimes metal goods. These exchanges, though controlled by border officials, helped certain northern towns grow.

6.8 Unrest and Uprisings

As the 19th century progressed, corruption and mismanagement grew in many local offices. Heavy taxes and forced labor demands angered peasants. Natural disasters, like floods or droughts, added to their struggles. Famine could push people to desperation, causing theft or protests.

Some peasants formed secret groups to fight back. They attacked government granaries or mansions of corrupt officials. These uprisings were often small and quickly crushed by the army. Still, they revealed deep anger in the countryside, including the north. Leaders of these revolts sometimes claimed a new era of justice was coming, drawing on folk religion or even rumored prophecies.

One of the better-known rebellions in the late 19th century was the **Donghak Peasant Movement**, though its major battles took place mostly in the southern regions. Yet, news of such uprisings traveled far, inspiring some northern communities to consider their own forms of resistance if oppression grew worse.

6.9 The Role of Regent Heungseon Daewongun (1860s–1870s)

In the mid-19th century, power in the Joseon royal court shifted when King Gojong was still too young to rule. His father, Heungseon Daewongun (often called Daewongun for short), acted as regent and tried to strengthen the monarchy:

1. **Centralizing Power**

   - The Daewongun reduced the influence of key factions in the government. He tried to limit the power of the yangban class that had grown too comfortable.

   - He closed some private Confucian academies, blaming them for supporting factional politics.

2. **Tax Reforms and Construction**

   - He tried to collect taxes more fairly, though corruption did not vanish overnight.

   - He spent resources to rebuild the Gyeongbok Palace in the capital, a grand project that required high taxes and labor from the provinces, including the north.

3. **Isolation Policy**

   - The Daewongun fiercely opposed opening up to foreign countries.

   - He also punished those who adopted Western religions or ideas, seeing them as threats to Confucian values.

While this chapter focuses on society rather than modern foreign interventions, it is worth noting that Daewongun's strict policies affected how the north was governed. Tax burdens rose again, sparking local discontent. Garrison towns had to contribute labor and money for palace rebuilding. Some of the improvements he introduced ended up adding stress to northern villagers who were already struggling.

6.10 Western Influences Begin to Appear

Although Joseon tried hard to remain isolated, some Western influence trickled in through China or occasional foreign ships. Catholic missionaries had been secretly entering Joseon since the late 18th century, converting a few people in different provinces.

In the north, contact with the Qing Dynasty sometimes brought Western books or goods that Qing merchants had picked up from European traders. Local scholars who saw these items grew curious about ideas like Western astronomy, medicine, or machines. But the government generally viewed such knowledge as dangerous. Officials feared it could weaken Confucian beliefs or invite foreign intrusion.

While we are not focusing on modern times, it is important to note that these small hints of Western culture created more debate within Joseon about whether the kingdom should open up to the outside or stay closed. This tension added another layer to the social shifts already happening.

6.11 The Spread of New Religious Movements

Besides Catholicism, other new religious ideas emerged in the 19th century:

- **Donghak ("Eastern Learning")**: A spiritual movement mixing Confucian, Buddhist, Taoist, and shamanistic elements. It taught that all people have the divine within them.
- **Various Millenarian Sects**: Groups predicting an upcoming age of peace, sometimes led by a charismatic figure claiming special powers.

These movements often appealed to peasants frustrated by heavy taxes and social injustice. Some leaders promised a fairer society or heavenly protection from suffering. The court saw these groups as rebels or heretics. In the north, such teachings sometimes spread quietly in remote villages, where government control was weaker.

6.12 Local Officials and Reformist Ideas

Toward the late 19th century, a few local administrators in the north began trying new policies:

- **Improved Infrastructure**: Some built roads or small bridges to help farmers get their goods to market.
- **Local Schools**: They set up Confucian-based village schools so children could learn reading, writing, and basic ethics.
- **Fairer Tax Collection**: They attempted to track farmland more accurately, reducing double taxation or bribery.

These efforts were small and faced resistance from traditional elites or corrupt officers. Still, they showed that even within a strict system, there were officials who wanted to make daily life better for common folks.

6.13 Natural Disasters and Famines

The north was often hit by severe winters and occasional droughts or floods:

1. **Crop Failures**

    - A bad year could wipe out entire fields of grain.

    - Farming families with little surplus risked starvation.

2. **Migration**

    - If famine struck, some people migrated to other provinces or across the border into Qing territory, seeking food or work.

    - This led to lost labor at home and a loss of community stability.

3. **Government Relief**

    - The court kept emergency grain stores called **uhyangchang** in theory, but corruption often meant these stores were empty or sold off.

    - In better-managed areas, local governors distributed grain loans or opened public works so peasants could earn food.

Famine had huge effects on society, weakening trust in the government if it failed to help. Stories of neglect traveled fast, fueling unrest.

6.14 Rise of Regional Identity

Through all these hardships, people in the north developed a sense of shared identity based on their frontier challenges:

- **Ties to Goguryeo**: Some families told stories of ancient Goguryeo times, taking pride in living on land once ruled by powerful northern kings.
- **Frontier Spirit**: The harsh climate and frequent threats bred resilience. Village communities often worked together in ways that might not have been as necessary in milder southern regions.
- **Trade Connections**: Northern traders who dealt with Qing merchants or carried goods south had broader views than some closed-off local communities. This gave them a sense of being part of a larger network.

This growing regional consciousness did not usually manifest as open separation from Joseon, but it did give people a sense that they were different from those in the more comfortable south.

6.15 Late 19th-Century Stirrings

By the mid-to-late 19th century, Joseon's struggles were becoming more obvious:

1. **Corruption and Power Games**

    - Court officials, regents, and royal in-laws often fought for control, draining resources.

    - Northern governors changed frequently due to court intrigues, making consistent policy hard to maintain.

2. **International Pressures**

    - Western powers, along with Japan and Russia, looked for ways to influence or access Joseon. Although we will not dive into modern developments, their presence became more apparent.

    - The north, bordering both China and Russia, felt new pressures as foreign interests in Manchuria grew.

3. **Peasant Grievances**

    - Suffering from repeated taxes, forced labor, and famine, many peasants in the north were ready to revolt if given a spark.

    - Some found hope in new religious or political movements promising relief and social equality.

Against this backdrop, the Joseon court attempted limited reforms, but often they were too little and too late. The stage was set for bigger changes that would come with the opening of Korea's ports, the rise of foreign influence, and eventually the downfall of the Joseon Dynasty itself in the early 20th century.

6.16 Cultural Achievements and Folklore

While politics and hardships can dominate the story, the Late Joseon Period also saw cultural flowering:

- **Literature**: Popular novels in Hangul, such as "Heungbujeon" or "Tale of Hong Gildong," circulated among common people. They often featured heroes from humble backgrounds and taught lessons about fairness and morality.
- **Folktales and Songs**: In northern villages, people shared stories around the fireplace during long winters. These tales spoke of spirits in the mountains or river gods, mixing local legends with bits of history.
- **Art and Music**: Confucian ceremonies and folk festivals both had music and dance. Pansori, a form of musical storytelling, gained popularity, though it was more established in the southern regions.

Many of these cultural forms provided comfort and entertainment, helping people endure tough times. They also strengthened a shared identity, bonding communities through common stories and traditions.

6.17 Approaching the Twilight of Joseon

As the 19th century drew to a close, Joseon faced major challenges that signaled an end to the old ways:

1. **Economic Problems**: Debt, misused taxes, and failing crops eroded trust in the monarchy.
2. **Social Tensions**: Class boundaries had begun to shift. Some peasants dared to question yangban authority.
3. **Weak Military**: Despite earlier reforms, the army was outdated compared to modern forces that foreign powers could bring to bear.
4. **External Interests**: Japan, Russia, and Western countries had their eyes on Joseon for strategic or commercial reasons, leading to future conflicts and treaties.

These issues set the stage for a series of dramatic events that would occur as the 20th century approached. Although we will not explore modern times deeply here, it is important to understand that Late Joseon's internal problems weakened the kingdom, making it vulnerable to foreign pressure.

6.18 Conclusion

The Late Joseon Period was a time of both growth and struggle. Reforms under enlightened kings improved some aspects of society, while agriculture and trade brought modest prosperity to certain regions, including parts of the north. However, corruption, natural disasters, and ongoing power struggles took a heavy toll on peasants.

Northern communities continued to adapt to harsh winters, border uncertainties, and shifting trade conditions. They maintained folk traditions and beliefs, balancing them with Confucian ideals promoted by the government. Over time, the strain of taxes, forced labor, and official neglect led to scattered uprisings, showing deep unrest below the kingdom's surface.

As Joseon neared the end of the 19th century, its future looked uncertain. Reforms were not enough to fix the underlying problems, and new foreign influences were knocking at the gates. In our next chapters, we will see how outside forces and internal changes combined to push Korea toward a new era, eventually shaping the path that led to the country we now call North Korea.

CHAPTER 7

EARLY FOREIGN INFLUENCES AND KOREA'S OPENING

Introduction

By the mid-19th century, Korea was still under Joseon rule. The kingdom had faced invasions, internal struggles, and social changes over many centuries. Yet, a new kind of challenge was emerging: foreign powers knocking at Korea's doors. Western nations, as well as neighboring countries like Japan and Russia, were becoming more interested in Korea for trade, resources, or strategic reasons.

In this chapter, we will explore how foreign influences began to shape the peninsula before the official annexation by Japan in 1910. We will see how missionaries, merchants, and diplomats tried to enter Korea, how the Joseon court reacted, and why the northern regions played a special role during this time. We will discuss treaties that forced Korea to open its ports, the push-and-pull between staying isolated or embracing new ideas, and the effects on ordinary people's lives. By looking at these events, we can better understand why Korea's society and government had to change so quickly in the late 1800s and early 1900s.

7.1 The "Hermit Kingdom" Policy

For many years, Joseon had tried to keep a policy of isolation. The government, influenced by Confucian ideals, believed in careful control of outside contact. They feared foreign religions like Catholicism, which was called "Western Learning," and viewed Western traders as a threat to Joseon's traditions and security.

This approach earned Korea the nickname "Hermit Kingdom" among Westerners. It meant the country shut its doors to most foreigners. But complete isolation was not truly possible. Joseon still had tributary relations with the Qing Dynasty in China, and it had small-scale trade or diplomatic links with Japan. Also, some Western knowledge slipped in through China, like books on science or geography that had been translated into Chinese.

Yet, the Joseon court remained cautious. Local officials were told to watch the coasts for foreign ships, and people caught spreading Christianity or other foreign beliefs could face harsh punishment. This tension between wanting to stay closed and needing to interact with the outside world set the stage for major changes.

7.2 Early Encounters with Western Ships

Starting in the 17th and 18th centuries, European and American ships occasionally landed on Korea's shores, sometimes by accident. Sailors from these ships were looking for trade or a safe place to fix a damaged vessel. Most of these encounters were small and did not lead to big changes. Local officials often turned the foreigners away or kept them under watch until they left.

Over time, however, Western nations grew stronger in East Asia. The Opium Wars in China (mid-19th century) showed how powerful Western armies and navies could be. Some Korean scholars realized that if Western powers forced open China's ports, they might soon do the same to Korea. Their warnings often fell on deaf ears in the royal court, which hoped the kingdom's isolation and small size would protect it.

When a few Western ships arrived asking for treaties or trade, they were usually rejected. For example, in 1866 a French mission came seeking to end persecution of Korean Catholics. After it was turned down, a French fleet attacked Ganghwa Island, although they did not succeed in fully invading. A few years later, in 1871, a U.S. expedition came to seek trade and punish Korea for earlier clashes. These incidents, while minor in scale, proved that foreign nations were willing to use force.

7.3 Internal Pressures and the Daewongun's Isolation

During the 1860s and early 1870s, Heungseon Daewongun (the regent for the young King Gojong) enforced a strict isolation policy. He believed that opening to foreign powers would destroy Joseon's Confucian values and independence. He also cracked down on Christians, both foreign missionaries and local converts, in an attempt to wipe out "dangerous" beliefs.

His harsh measures kept most foreigners away for a time, but they also caused tension. Some members of the royal court began to doubt that total isolation was wise, especially after seeing China's defeats at Western hands. They quietly discussed the idea of limited reforms, including learning Western technology, so Joseon could strengthen its defense.

In the north, life continued as before in many ways. Yet the region was not entirely cut off from new ideas. Traders going back and forth to Qing territory sometimes carried stories or small goods from the West, which they had seen in Chinese markets. A few local scholars in the north heard about modern inventions like steamships or rifles, fueling curiosity about how such technology could impact Korea's security.

7.4 The Ganghwa Treaty (1876) with Japan

One major turning point came in 1876, when Japan forced Joseon to sign the Treaty of Ganghwa. By then, Japan had undergone its own transformation with the Meiji Restoration, adopting Western-style armies, navies, and industries. Armed with modern ships, Japan approached Korea and demanded it open ports for trade.

1. **Terms of the Treaty**

    - Korea had to open three ports to Japanese commerce.

    - Japan gained "extraterritorial rights," meaning Japanese citizens in Korea were subject to Japanese law, not Korean law.

- Japan recognized Korea as an "independent" state, which actually reduced Qing China's claim over the peninsula.

2. **Effects on Joseon**

    - The treaty was very one-sided, favoring Japan.

    - It led to the arrival of Japanese merchants who set up shops in opened port cities.

    - Some Korean officials saw the need to update the military and economy to compete with Japan.

The Ganghwa Treaty signaled the start of Korea's forced opening. Soon, other countries like the United States, Britain, and Russia demanded similar deals, each wanting trade advantages. Although these treaties were signed by the royal court, many Koreans felt uneasy about the sudden influx of foreigners and foreign goods.

7.5 Modernization Efforts and the Northern Role

With the door now partly open, the royal court realized that some modernization might be needed to preserve independence. King Gojong, taking full power after the Daewongun's regency ended, listened to a few reform-minded officials. They proposed sending students and envoys abroad to learn Western military training, industry, and governmental systems.

- **Military Upgrades**: Joseon purchased modern rifles and cannons. Foreign instructors, often from Japan or the West, were hired to train new Korean army units.
- **Schools and Language**: Some new schools began teaching subjects like math, science, and foreign languages. While these were mostly in Seoul, a handful of local officials in the north also tried to bring modern lessons to bigger towns.

- **Industry**: Small attempts at building factories started, though progress was slow due to lack of funds and the strong Confucian mindset that valued agriculture over industry.

The north remained somewhat on the sidelines of these efforts, as the capital preferred to focus on coastal and central regions. However, local leaders in the north saw a chance to request more roads or telegraph lines, hoping improved infrastructure would help defend against future threats from across the northern border.

7.6 Competing Foreign Interests: Qing, Japan, and Russia

Joseon's new openness also meant competing foreign powers could vie for influence in Korea:

1. **Qing China**

    - As Joseon's longstanding "elder brother," Qing China wanted to keep Korea under its sphere of influence.

    - After the Ganghwa Treaty, the Qing tried to reassert control by sending advisors and influencing the Korean court.

2. **Japan**

    - Japan aimed to expand its political and economic reach.

    - Japanese officials and merchants set up offices in port cities, offering loans and deals that often benefited Japan more than Korea.

3. **Russia**

    - Russia had interest in a warm-water port and wanted to extend its influence down through Manchuria to the Korean Peninsula.

- Some Koreans saw Russia as a possible ally to counterbalance Japan, but others feared Russian expansionism.

These power struggles often happened in Seoul, where foreign legations (diplomatic offices) were established. But the effects rippled outward. Northern regions, close to Russian territory via Manchuria, sometimes worried about Russian explorers or soldiers who might cross the border.

7.7 The Rise of Reform Movements

Inside Korea, different groups had varied opinions on how to respond to foreign pressures and modernization:

- **Conservative Faction**: Wanted to stick to Confucian traditions and limit foreign influence. They saw Western ideas as dangerous to Joseon's moral fabric.
- **Enlightenment Faction** (Gaehwa Party): Favored learning from the West and Japan to strengthen Korea's economy and military. They argued that adopting new technology was the only way to protect the kingdom from colonization.

Tensions between these factions led to political turmoil. At times, members of the Enlightenment Faction tried to stage coups or major reforms, only to be put down by conservatives allied with the Qing or other powerful groups.

7.8 The Northern Response: Balancing Old and New

In northern provinces, common people were often less aware of the detailed court politics but could see certain changes:

- **Arrival of Modern Goods**: Japanese traders sometimes brought modern textiles, tools, or even kerosene lamps. Local markets saw new items, sparking curiosity but also suspicion.
- **Missionary Presence**: Some Christian missionaries, especially Protestants, traveled quietly through northern towns. They set up small churches, schools, or clinics. Locals were sometimes attracted by the free education or medical help.
- **Local Officials' Dilemma**: They had to follow orders from Seoul, but also deal with local concerns about new ideas. If they appeared too friendly to foreigners, they risked angering conservative nobles. If they were too strict, they might miss the chance to modernize and improve the region.

Overall, the north tried to adapt at its own pace, keeping up some old frontier traditions while slowly absorbing certain Western or Japanese influences.

7.9 Religious Changes and Education

The late 1800s saw a gradual spread of Christianity in Korea, both Catholic and Protestant. The Catholic Church had been in Korea underground for decades, but foreign priests still risked their lives to preach. In the 1880s, American Protestant missionaries arrived with permission from the court, focusing on schools and hospitals.

- **Schools**: Missionaries taught modern subjects like math, science, and foreign languages alongside religious lessons. Some northern families sent their children to these schools, hoping they would learn skills that might lead to better opportunities.
- **Hospitals**: Simple clinics run by missionaries offered basic Western medicine, treating diseases that local herbal remedies struggled to cure. This built goodwill in communities.
- **Conflicts**: Confucian scholars often opposed Christianity, claiming it disrupted ancestral rites and promoted "foreign gods." In some areas, new believers faced social rejection or even violence.

Despite challenges, these educational and medical efforts had a growing impact, especially in the north where official resources were scarce. People valued the new knowledge and care they received.

7.10 The Gapsin Coup (1884) and the Aftermath

One dramatic moment in Joseon's path to change was the Gapsin Coup of 1884. A group of young reformers, influenced by Japan, tried to seize the royal palace and push for rapid modernization. They wanted to set up a new government system, end certain noble privileges, and expand commerce.

- **Short-Lived Takeover**: The coup lasted only a few days.
- **Qing Intervention**: Qing troops quickly moved in to support the existing Joseon government.
- **Failure and Punishment**: The coup leaders fled to Japan or were executed.

This event showed how deep the divisions were among Koreans about foreign-inspired changes. It also signaled that Qing China would step in if Joseon moved too close to Japan. For the north, the coup itself had little direct impact, but it contributed to the overall tension that shaped national policies.

7.11 Donghak Peasant Uprising (1894) and Northern Reactions

Another key turning point was the Donghak Peasant Uprising (1894). Donghak ("Eastern Learning") was a religious and social movement that sought fairness for peasants and an end to foreign domination. It mixed spiritual ideas with calls for social reform. Though the major battles were in the southern regions, the ideas spread widely:

1. **Goals of the Uprising**

    - Reduce heavy taxes and punish corrupt local officials.
    - Expel foreign powers that were harming the country.
    - Promote equal treatment of all classes.

2. **Impact on the North**

    - Some northern peasants, tired of oppression, sympathized with the rebellion's goals.
    - However, local authorities acted quickly to prevent large-scale uprisings. They warned that supporting rebels would bring severe punishment.

3. **Outcome**

    - The court asked both Qing and Japanese forces to help quell the rebellion, leading to the First Sino-Japanese War (1894–1895) fought mainly on Korean soil.
    - Japan's victory over China further weakened Qing influence in Korea, paving the way for Japan to gain more control.

For northern communities, the turmoil meant continued uncertainty. They watched foreign armies move through parts of the country, and they heard rumors of battles and shifting power in Seoul. Many people just hoped for stability and enough food to survive, as they had for generations.

7.12 First Sino-Japanese War and Its Consequences

Japan's victory in the First Sino-Japanese War was a massive blow to the Qing Dynasty. It ended the longtime idea that China was the main protector of Korea. Under the Treaty of Shimonoseki (1895):

- **Qing Lost Control**: China recognized Korea as a fully independent state.
- **Japan's Influence Rose**: Japan gained Taiwan and other territories, boosting its confidence.
- **Korean Reforms**: Japan pushed King Gojong's court to implement more reforms, often called the "Gabo Reforms," aimed at modernizing government, laws, and social customs.

These reforms included ending the civil service exam based solely on Confucian classics, shifting to a more modern police and judicial system, and trying to reorganize local administration. Still, corruption and resistance slowed actual progress, and many conservative officials viewed Japan's meddling with distrust.

7.13 The Assassination of Queen Min (1895)

One of the most tragic events of this period was the assassination of Queen Min, also known as Empress Myeongseong, in 1895. She had become a key figure in the court, leaning toward Russian support as a counterweight to Japan's growing power. Japanese officials and their Korean allies saw her as an obstacle to their goals.

- **Attack on the Palace**: A group of Japanese agents and pro-Japanese Korean troops broke into the palace, killing the queen.
- **Public Outrage**: News of this brutal act shocked Koreans, fueling anti-Japanese sentiment.
- **King Gojong's Flight**: Fearing for his own safety, King Gojong later took refuge in the Russian legation in Seoul for about a year.

The murder of Queen Min deepened divisions in society. Some in the north heard about her death and became more fearful of Japan's intentions, suspecting that Japan would stop at nothing to control Joseon. This suspicion would grow in the coming years.

7.14 Russo-Japanese Rivalry and the Northern Border

After China's defeat, Russia became the next major power vying for influence in Korea. The northern border with Russia was of special concern. Russians had built outposts near the Amur River region and looked with interest at Korea's warm-water ports.

- **Russian Advisors**: King Gojong invited some Russian advisors to help modernize the army and to counterbalance Japan.
- **Japanese Reaction**: Japan saw Russia's presence in Korea as a direct threat to its own expansion.

This rivalry eventually led to the Russo-Japanese War (1904–1905). While most fighting took place in Manchuria and at sea, Korea was pulled into the conflict as both sides moved troops through the peninsula. After Japan triumphed, it forced Korea to sign new agreements that gave Japan near-complete control over Korean affairs.

7.15 King Gojong's Attempts at Survival

Facing intense pressure from Japan and wary of Russia's intentions, King Gojong tried a variety of moves to keep Korea independent:

- **Proclaiming the Korean Empire (Daehan Empire) in 1897**: Gojong declared himself Emperor, aiming to show Korea was a sovereign empire, no longer a tributary of China.
- **Modernization Steps**: He encouraged building telegraph lines, a railway system, modern postal services, and even Western-style schools.
- **International Appeals**: Gojong sent envoys to Western nations, hoping for support against Japanese aggression. However, these efforts met limited success because the major powers were focused on their own interests in Asia.

In the north, local officials tried to follow the new imperial rules, but real changes were slow. A few telegraph lines and roads were built. Some private missionaries or entrepreneurs started small businesses, like spinning mills or brick factories. Yet, most northern farmers still struggled with the same daily issues of harsh winters, small plots of land, and uncertain markets.

7.16 Japan's Growing Grip: The Protectorate Treaty (1905)

After winning the Russo-Japanese War, Japan forced Korea to sign the Eulsa Treaty in 1905. This made Korea a protectorate of Japan, meaning Japan took over Korea's foreign affairs and placed advisors in key government positions. Many Koreans, including high officials, protested, but the treaty was imposed by force.

1. **Loss of Sovereignty**

    - Korea could no longer conduct its own diplomacy.
    - Japanese advisors effectively controlled major policies.

2. **Public Reaction**

    - Anger spread among the Korean people.
    - Some officials resigned in protest. Some took their own lives in an act of defiance.
    - Secret societies formed, planning ways to resist Japanese influence.

In the north, patriotic gatherings took place in certain towns, with local leaders urging people to speak out. However, open resistance was dangerous, as Japanese agents kept watch for troublemakers.

7.17 Toward Full Annexation (1910)

Over the next few years, Japan tightened its hold. It set up a Resident-General in Seoul, who overshadowed Korea's own officials. King Gojong was forced to step down in 1907 in favor of his son, Sunjong, who had even less power. Meanwhile, Japanese-run police stations spread across the country, and Japanese soldiers were stationed in key areas.

Military Disbandment

- One major blow was the disbanding of the Korean Army in 1907. Soldiers who lost their jobs often joined resistance groups, especially in mountainous regions like the north, to continue fighting as guerrillas.

Economic Intrusion

- Japanese companies purchased land and built railways, planning to extract natural resources and open markets for Japanese goods.
- Farmers who lost their land sometimes moved to Manchuria or tried to find work in new factories.

Finally, in 1910, Japan proclaimed the formal annexation of Korea. With this, the country became a colony of the Japanese Empire, and the Joseon Dynasty officially ended after over five centuries of rule.

CHAPTER 8

JAPANESE OCCUPATION (1910–1945)

Introduction

In 1910, Korea was annexed by Japan. This began a 35-year period of colonial rule that would transform the peninsula. During this time, Koreans lost direct control of their government, schools, and economy. The Japanese authorities imposed policies that aimed to assimilate Koreans into the Japanese Empire. Resistance movements arose, both at home and abroad.

In this chapter, we will explore how Japan ruled Korea during these colonial years and how it affected everyday life, especially in the north. We will look at changes in agriculture, industry, education, and culture. We will also see how Korean nationalism grew stronger under oppression, leading to protests and underground organizations. Although open rebellion was dangerous, many Koreans found ways to keep their identity alive. This sets the stage for the conflicts that followed the end of World War II, which we will cover in later chapters.

8.1 The Early Years of Colonial Rule

Right after the annexation, Japan installed a Governor-General in Seoul with broad powers. All significant decisions about law, order, and economic development came from this office. Korean officials who once served the Joseon court were pushed aside or given minor roles.

Key Features of Early Rule

1. **Military Police System**: Japan stationed many police and soldiers throughout the country. Dissent was quickly suppressed.

2. **Land Survey**: A large-scale land survey began in 1910, forcing Koreans to register their property. Some lost their rights due to confusing paperwork or corruption, ending up as tenant farmers on land they once owned.
3. **Censorship and Control**: Newspapers, books, and public gatherings needed official approval. Any hint of anti-Japanese sentiment was banned or punished.

In the north, these measures felt even more intrusive because local communities, used to some autonomy, now faced sudden oversight by Japanese police. Farmers had to prove ownership of their fields in a new legal system, and those who failed could lose everything.

8.2 Economic Exploitation

One of Japan's goals was to use Korea's resources to fuel its own rapid industrial growth. This involved:

- **Agricultural Production**: Korean rice was shipped to Japan to feed its growing population. Some farmland was converted to cash crops, like cotton, which Japan needed for its textile factories.
- **Mining and Forestry**: In the mountainous north, Japanese companies mined coal, iron, and other minerals. Forests were also cut down for timber.
- **Infrastructure Development**: Railways, roads, and ports were built, not mainly to help Koreans, but to transport resources to Japan more efficiently.

While some Koreans found work in these new projects, wages were usually low and working conditions harsh. Japanese owners and investors reaped most of the profits. Over time, rural poverty grew, pushing many northern farmers to look for jobs in mines or factories, or even to migrate elsewhere, such as Manchuria.

8.3 Forced Cultural Assimilation

To tighten control, the colonial government introduced policies aimed at erasing or minimizing Korean culture:

1. **Japanese Language**: School lessons and official documents were increasingly done in Japanese. Korean students had to learn Japanese history and customs.
2. **Soshi-kaimei ("Name-changing")**: Koreans were pressured to adopt Japanese-style names, especially after 1939.
3. **Banning Traditions**: Traditional Korean rituals, clothing styles, and even newspapers in Korean were restricted or discouraged.

These measures aimed to turn Koreans into loyal subjects of the Japanese Emperor. In northern towns, teachers who spoke the local dialect or used Korean textbooks found themselves replaced by Japanese staff or forced to comply with new rules. Public signs and announcements switched to Japanese, making it harder for older Koreans who never learned the language.

8.4 The March First Movement (1919)

Despite the heavy-handed rule, resistance grew. On March 1, 1919, a peaceful protest for Korean independence erupted in Seoul and spread across the nation. Koreans gathered to read a Declaration of Independence, written by intellectuals and religious leaders.

- **Nationwide Protests**: Hundreds of thousands of people in cities and villages took part. They marched, waved flags, and called for freedom.
- **Violent Suppression**: The Japanese police and army responded with force, arresting, beating, and killing many demonstrators.
- **Impact**: Although it did not end colonial rule, the March First Movement sparked greater national consciousness. It also drew international attention to Korea's plight.

In the north, people joined marches in towns like Pyongyang, Anju, and Sinuiju. Mission schools and churches sometimes became centers of protest, as they had contacts with global organizations that might support the cause of Korean independence. Though many protestors were jailed or worse, the spirit of unity spread widely, planting seeds for future resistance.

8.5 Changes in Japanese Policy After 1919

Stunned by the scale of the March First Movement, the Japanese government decided to soften some of its policies, a shift sometimes called the "Cultural Policy." This meant:

- **Easier Censorship Rules**: A few Korean-language newspapers and magazines were allowed, though still monitored.
- **Limited Self-Expression**: Korean cultural events were sometimes permitted, as long as they did not challenge colonial authority.
- **Reforms in Schools**: Korean language classes reappeared, though Japanese remained dominant.

However, these changes were limited. Real power stayed firmly in Japanese hands, and any open talk of independence was still met with harsh punishment. In the north, some local clubs or literary groups emerged, trying to keep Korean traditions alive under the watchful eye of Japanese police.

8.6 The Rise of Nationalist and Socialist Groups

During the 1920s and 1930s, various groups formed to fight colonial rule or to argue for social change in Korea:

1. **Nationalist Parties**: These groups wanted independence from Japan, often looking to Western ideas about democracy. They published newspapers and held secret meetings.

2. **Socialist/Communist Circles**: Some Koreans, inspired by the Russian Revolution of 1917, believed socialism or communism could free them from both colonial rule and social injustice.
3. **Christian Organizations**: Churches in the north often acted as safe spaces for organizing, because they had networks that extended beyond Korea.

The colonial government suppressed all political activity that challenged its authority. Underground movements took root in northern cities and rural areas, as some leaders found it easier to hide in less monitored frontier districts or mountainous regions. A few went across the border into Manchuria or the Soviet Far East to link up with other Korean exiles.

8.7 Industrial Development in the North

While the south of Korea saw growth in light industries like textiles, the north became more of a center for heavy industry under Japanese rule:

- **Mining**: Coal, iron ore, and other minerals were extracted, especially in the northern provinces.
- **Hydroelectric Power**: Japan built dams on northern rivers to generate electricity for factories.
- **Metal and Chemical Plants**: Some major industrial complexes arose, employing thousands of workers, many of them Koreans under strict supervision.

Though these industries brought jobs, working conditions were tough. Laborers worked long hours with low pay, and they had little freedom to organize or protest. Many factory owners were Japanese, keeping the higher-paying administrative and technical roles for themselves. Koreans were generally limited to lower-tier positions.

Despite the hardships, some Koreans in the north learned valuable skills, like operating machinery or managing modern industrial processes. This knowledge would later play a role in post-colonial economic developments, though that story lies beyond our immediate history focus.

8.8 Everyday Life Under Colonial Rule

For ordinary people, colonial rule reshaped daily routines:

1. **Taxes and Forced Labor**: Farmers gave up large portions of their harvest to meet high tax demands. Some were forced to work on construction projects, like roads or railways, often without fair pay.
2. **Education System**: Children went to schools where the curriculum pushed loyalty to Japan. Many Korean children either dropped out early or did not attend, helping instead on farms or in family businesses.
3. **Social Restrictions**: Koreans had to bow to Japanese officials, speak politely in Japanese, and adopt Japanese manners in public offices.
4. **Loss of Cultural Identity**: People had to be cautious about wearing traditional hanbok or practicing Korean customs in public, especially after assimilation policies tightened in the 1930s.

In northern provinces, the rugged terrain and distance from the colonial capital in Seoul sometimes gave communities a bit more breathing room. Yet, Japanese police posts were set up in most major towns, ensuring that the authorities could respond quickly to suspected "rebellious" activities.

8.9 Migration and Manchuria

Because of the harsh conditions at home, many Koreans chose or were forced to move, particularly to Manchuria:

- **Farming Opportunities**: Some families believed they could find cheaper land or better prospects across the border.
- **Escape from Oppression**: Others fled to avoid Japanese police or forced labor.
- **Labor Demand**: Factories and mines in Manchuria, owned by Japanese or Chinese companies, hired Koreans as a cheap workforce.

These migrant communities kept their Korean identity alive. Some also became involved in independence movements, linking up with anti-Japanese forces in China or in the Soviet Union. Stories of bandit groups or freedom fighters operating along the border spread among northern villagers, feeding hopes that liberation could come from outside.

8.10 Cultural Movements and Literature

Despite oppression, Korean culture did not vanish. Writers, poets, and artists found subtle ways to express national pride or critique colonial rule:

- **Literature**: Some novels and poems highlighted the struggles of ordinary Koreans. Writers used symbolic language to avoid direct censorship.
- **Theater and Music**: Plays and musical performances sometimes included hidden messages of resistance. Traditional music like pansori found new audiences as a way to keep Korean heritage alive.
- **Newspapers**: Korean-language publications (closely monitored) featured articles on social issues, education, and sometimes, gentle criticisms of certain policies.

In the north, Christian missions and local study groups often doubled as cultural circles. They taught literacy in Hangul and shared old legends or historical stories about Korea's past greatness. Younger Koreans who felt a strong sense of national identity were inspired to keep their traditions alive, even if it had to be done quietly.

8.11 The 1930s: Increasing Militarization

During the 1930s, Japan became more militaristic. It invaded Manchuria in 1931 and soon launched full-scale war in China. The colonial government in Korea shifted gears, demanding total support for Japan's war efforts:

- **Resource Extraction**: More minerals, food supplies, and manpower were taken from Korea.
- **Military Recruitment**: Koreans were pressed into service as laborers, and later, men were drafted into the Japanese army.
- **Emperor Worship**: Schools and offices began daily rituals venerating the Japanese Emperor. Korean children had to bow toward the Imperial Palace in Tokyo.

These policies intensified assimilation. By the late 1930s, speaking Korean at schools or in official places could result in punishment. The name-changing campaign (Soshi-kaimei) forced Koreans to adopt Japanese surnames. Many resisted in private, but open defiance was dangerous.

8.12 Women's Suffering: "Comfort Women"

One of the darkest aspects of colonial rule was the forced recruitment of Korean women into sexual slavery for the Japanese military. They were euphemistically called "comfort women." While not limited to the north, it affected women across Korea:

- **False Promises**: Some were told they would work in factories or restaurants abroad, only to be taken to military "comfort stations."

- **Horrible Conditions**: These women were abused by soldiers and forced to live in captivity.
- **Silence and Shame**: After the war, many survivors felt unable to speak about their experiences for decades.

This tragic chapter highlights the extreme abuses under Japanese imperialism. The stories of these women would only come to wider public attention long after colonial rule ended.

8.13 Growing Resistance: Guerrilla Groups

Not all resistance took the form of peaceful protests. Some Koreans took up arms:

- **Armed Fighters in Manchuria**: Small guerrilla bands, including some led by future North Korean leaders, operated along the border. They carried out raids on Japanese positions or supply lines.
- **Soviet Partisans**: A few Korean exiles joined Soviet partisan groups, hoping to strike at Japan from the north.
- **Risk at Home**: Operating inside Korea was very dangerous, so many armed fighters stayed outside official borders, relying on supportive local networks.

Though these groups were never large enough to overthrow Japanese rule alone, they kept the spirit of armed resistance alive. Stories of these fighters occasionally reached northern villages, inspiring hope but also fear of Japanese retaliation.

8.14 Wartime Mobilization (1937–1945)

When Japan expanded its war across the Pacific after 1937, colonial Korea was pulled even deeper into the conflict:

- **Conscription**: Korean men were drafted into the Japanese military. Some were sent to battlefields in China, Southeast Asia, or the Pacific Islands.

- **Forced Labor**: Factories ran at full capacity to support Japan's war machine. Young Koreans, both men and women, were made to work long hours.
- **Rationing and Hardship**: Food and goods became scarce. Families faced hunger and disease as resources were diverted to the Japanese war effort.

In the north, heavy industry was further expanded, with mines and plants operating under strict rules. Many local workers were recruited or forced to move to bigger industrial sites, living in cramped dormitories. Any talk against the war was treated as treason.

8.15 Effects on Local Culture and Identity

Over three decades of colonial rule, Korean identity was deeply challenged, but it did not disappear:

1. **Clan Traditions**: Extended families in rural areas quietly kept Korean customs, like ancestral rites and traditional festivals, often behind closed doors.
2. **Hangul Preservation**: Even when schools banned it, people taught their children Hangul at home or through church groups.
3. **Secret Societies**: Some intellectuals met in private, reading Korean history or literature to keep the past alive.
4. **Religious Havens**: Christian churches and Buddhist temples could act as shelters for patriotic feeling, provided they avoided direct confrontation with Japanese authorities.

In the north, these cultural ties remained strong, partly due to tight-knit communities in towns and villages. The mountainous terrain also offered refuge for secret gatherings.

8.16 Paths to Independence: International Context

Toward the end of World War II, Japan's fortunes changed. The Allied Powers, including the United States and the Soviet Union, advanced against Japanese forces in Asia and the Pacific. Koreans living abroad formed independence groups, lobbying Western governments to recognize Korea's right to be free after Japan's defeat:

- **Provisional Government of the Republic of Korea**: Established in Shanghai in 1919, it worked with various world leaders to gain support, though results were limited.
- **Allied Declarations**: The Cairo Declaration (1943) and the Potsdam Declaration (1945) mentioned the future independence of Korea, giving hope to Koreans under Japanese rule.
- **Soviet Advance in Manchuria**: By 1945, Soviet troops were pushing into Manchuria, bringing them close to the Korean border.

As the war drew to a close, many Koreans anticipated Japan's imminent defeat. Underground activists and resistance fighters prepared for the moment they could rise up or return home to claim freedom.

8.17 Liberation (August 15, 1945)

Japan's surrender in August 1945 ended the colonial period. Koreans celebrated "Gwangbokjeol," meaning "Restoration of Light," on August 15. The sudden collapse of Japanese authority left a power vacuum. People tore down Japanese signs, replaced them with Korean flags, and welcomed independence.

- **Immediate Euphoria**: Many marched in the streets, singing patriotic songs and hugging strangers.
- **Challenges**: However, there was no clear government ready to take over the entire country. Different political groups rushed to fill the void.
- **Northern Situation**: Soviet forces crossed into the north, while American forces landed in the south. This would set the stage for the peninsula's division.

Though full details of the post-liberation era go beyond this chapter, it is important to note that independence was not as simple as just regaining control. The seeds of division were already planted.

CHAPTER 9

GROWING NATIONALISM AND RESISTANCE MOVEMENTS

Introduction

From the early 20th century until the end of Japanese rule in 1945, Koreans faced strict controls in every part of life. Chapter 8 discussed how Japan took over the peninsula, imposed military policies, and tried to wipe out Korean identity. However, the Korean people did not simply accept these measures. Many formed groups—some open, many secret—to fight against colonial authority. These groups showed tremendous courage. They spread ideas about independence and national pride, despite constant threats of arrest or worse.

In this chapter, we look closely at the growth of Korean nationalism and the various resistance movements during the colonial era. We see that, within these efforts, the northern regions had a special role. They were close to Manchuria and Russia, which sometimes allowed fighters and activists to slip across borders for help. Christian churches, underground newspapers, and student clubs spread the message of independence, while farmers and factory workers joined labor unions to push back against colonial exploitation. Although Japan cracked down harshly, these movements laid the groundwork for Korea's eventual liberation. They also shaped the early leadership that would later be pivotal in forming what we know today as North Korea.

9.1 Early National Consciousness: Seeds of Resistance

Before the official annexation in 1910, many Koreans already disliked Japanese interference. However, true organized resistance grew stronger after the loss of sovereignty. Groups of intellectuals, religious leaders, and former government officials realized that if Korea did not act, it might lose its culture forever.

9.1.1 Reformist Thinkers

Some early reform-minded individuals, often inspired by the "enlightenment" trends of the late Joseon period, continued their calls for modernization as a way to stand up to Japan. Although many were silenced or forced to flee, they kept exchanging letters, pamphlets, and books about how other nations had resisted foreign rule.

9.1.2 Christian Influence

In the north, Christian churches, especially Protestant ones, played a strong part in teaching ideas of equality and hope. Pastors and church elders opened small schools, taught reading and writing in Hangul, and told their communities that all believers were brothers and sisters under God—an idea that clashed with the strict social hierarchy pushed by the Japanese. This sense of community often led to hidden gatherings where people discussed not just religion, but also independence.

9.1.3 Folk Traditions and Storytelling

Even outside organized religion or formal education, Koreans kept their sense of identity through folk songs, family histories, and old legends. Farmers in remote areas of the north, for example, passed on tales of ancient Goguryeo heroes who had once ruled the northern lands. These stories kept alive the memory that Koreans had their own glorious past.

Though these seeds of resistance were small, they planted ideas in people's minds: Korea had been independent once, and it could be again.

9.2 Underground Networks: Spreading Information and Hope

Under strict censorship, it was dangerous to speak openly against the Japanese government. Still, brave individuals formed secret circles to exchange banned newspapers or leaflets. In some cases, they used night schools or church gatherings as covers for meetings about independence.

9.2.1 Role of Students and Intellectuals

Young Koreans attending mission schools or private academies often learned about modern history, political thought, and global events. A few even traveled to China or Japan to study. There, they saw nationalist movements from other countries, giving them new strategies to apply back home.

- **Secret Clubs**: Inside schools, students organized small reading clubs. They read about world history, including how other nations had fought off colonizers.
- **Publishing Pamphlets**: These clubs wrote leaflets that described Korean culture, language, and history. Distributing these papers risked arrest, but it also awakened many people's sense of pride.

9.2.2 Local Markets and Traveling Merchants

In rural north, local markets were more than places to buy and sell goods. They became hubs of information. Traveling merchants might carry hidden messages or newspapers from one region to another. Villagers passing by could pick up rumors of new anti-Japanese activities or hear news about protests in other towns.

9.2.3 Church Gatherings and Night Schools

As mentioned, Christian gatherings offered some cover from Japanese surveillance. Pastors often emphasized moral teachings that inspired believers to see freedom as a basic right. Meanwhile, night schools—set up by both Christians and nationalists—taught reading and writing in Hangul. Students there learned that their language was key to preserving Korean identity. These lessons stoked the fire of resistance and gave people the literacy skills needed to read banned materials.

9.3 The Emergence of Organized Groups and Ideologies

Over time, as small circles grew bolder, they began to form bigger organizations. Different ideologies guided these groups, from moderate nationalism to more radical socialism or communism. Each offered a path to liberation from Japan, though they sometimes disagreed on methods.

9.3.1 Moderates and the Nationalist Movement

Moderate nationalists believed in peaceful change. They thought educating the population and appealing to global opinion could pressure Japan to leave. Some set up cultural societies that promoted the Korean language, ran adult literacy classes, and hosted patriotic events (when possible). They had to be subtle, though. A direct mention of "independence" could bring the colonial police.

9.3.2 Socialists and Communists

Inspired by the Russian Revolution in 1917, some Koreans concluded that overthrowing both foreign rule and local landlords was the solution. They saw capitalism as part of the colonial system that exploited workers. In the north, especially near the border with Manchuria and the Soviet Union, these ideas took hold among factory laborers and miners who faced harsh conditions.

- **Secret Cells**: Tiny cells of communists met secretly in factories or towns, spreading pamphlets about worker rights and urging strikes.
- **Cross-Border Networks**: A few activists traveled between Korea, Manchuria, and the Soviet Far East, gathering financial help or weapons for future uprisings.

These different streams of thought—moderate nationalism, Christian activism, and leftist ideologies—did not always work together smoothly. Yet, they shared a common enemy: Japanese colonial rule.

9.4 The March First Movement (1919) and Its Impact on the North

Chapter 8 described the March First Movement of 1919, a watershed moment in Korean resistance. Although it began in Seoul, it quickly spread throughout the peninsula, including the north. The event was a massive outcry for independence, fueled by years of suppressed anger.

9.4.1 Northern Protests

Cities like Pyongyang, Sinuiju, and Anju witnessed large gatherings. Christian churches were especially active in organizing rallies, as many pastors read the "Declaration of Independence" to their congregations. Students from local mission schools marched, carrying homemade flags and shouting slogans of freedom.

- **Harsh Crackdowns**: Japanese forces quickly responded. Leaders were arrested, and some protestors were beaten or shot. Nonetheless, the movement's scale showed that anti-colonial feelings ran deep.

9.4.2 Influence on Future Activism

Although the March First Movement was crushed, its spirit lived on. People who participated felt a renewed confidence: they had stood up publicly, joined hands with neighbors, and shouted for independence. Underground networks became more determined. The event also caught the world's attention, marking Korea's struggle as a genuine national movement.

9.4.3 Shifts in Japanese Policy

After 1919, Japan slightly relaxed its "military police" approach, shifting to a "cultural policy" that allowed a limited amount of Korean expression. However, true power still rested with the colonial government. But this brief easing gave breathing space for new cultural and political groups to form, some of which would continue pushing for independence.

9.5 Rise of Labor and Peasant Movements in the North

In the 1920s, Korea saw the growth of labor unions and peasant associations. The north, with its developing mines and factories, and with farmland often owned by absentee landlords, was fertile ground for worker and farmer activism.

9.5.1 Harsh Working Conditions

As Japanese companies expanded mining in the northern mountains, thousands of Koreans toiled in dangerous tunnels, extracting coal or iron ore. They worked long hours for low wages. Injuries and deaths were common. Factory labor was no better. In textile mills or metal workshops, workers faced strict discipline and frequent harassment from Japanese managers.

9.5.2 Labor Unions and Strikes

Secret labor unions emerged to demand better wages, shorter hours, and safer conditions. Organizers found inspiration in global labor movements. They produced leaflets that urged workers to stand together rather than submit to company rules.

- **Notable Strikes**: While smaller actions took place regularly, major strikes occasionally erupted, shaking local authorities. In some cases, thousands of workers walked off the job, paralyzing production until the Japanese police intervened.

9.5.3 Peasant Associations

Farmers in the north also struggled under high taxes, forced grain shipments, and landlord abuse. Some peasants formed associations or cooperatives to share resources and protest unfair rents. In certain villages, these groups had quiet support from teachers and religious figures who believed in social justice.

Though met with harsh suppression, such labor and peasant movements proved that resistance was not limited to intellectuals or students—it came from all walks of life.

9.6 Women in the Independence and Social Movements

Korean women, too, played key roles in resisting colonial rule. Traditional Korean society had often limited women's public roles, but this era of upheaval opened opportunities for them to become activists, educators, and organizers.

9.6.1 Women's Education

Mission schools for girls in the north taught them to read and write, which was previously less common. Educated women wrote articles about independence, women's rights, and social reform. Even if these writings had to be published secretly or in heavily censored magazines, they spread new ideas.

9.6.2 Underground Work

Some women served as couriers, smuggling documents or funds for resistance groups. Others helped shelter activists on the run. Their involvement was often overlooked, but without their support, many protests would have been impossible.

9.6.3 Famous Examples

The March First Movement saw several female leaders step forward. Figures like Yu Gwan-sun, though active more in the central regions, inspired women everywhere. In the north, lesser-known but equally brave women activists taught local girls about Korean history and culture, defying Japanese mandates to speak only Japanese in schools.

By claiming their place in public life, women in the north proved that the independence struggle belonged to everyone.

9.7 Exile Communities and Border Regions

One distinctive feature of northern resistance was the closeness to Manchuria and the Soviet Union. This gave some Koreans ways to slip across borders, where they set up exile communities or joined armed groups.

9.7.1 Manchurian Base Camps

A significant number of Koreans migrated to Manchuria—some looking for farmland, others fleeing Japanese oppression. Within these communities, independence activists formed schools, newspapers, and self-defense units. They held secret meetings to plan raids or gather supplies for fighters back in Korea.

9.7.2 Soviet Influence

After the Russian Revolution, the Soviet Union welcomed certain Korean activists who shared socialist ideals. A few leaders trained in Soviet military camps, learning guerrilla tactics. They hoped to return one day to drive out the Japanese with armed force.

- **Communist Ties**: Over time, these ties led to the rise of communist-minded independence fighters. Some figures who later became prominent in North Korean leadership emerged from these cross-border efforts.

9.7.3 Battles and Skirmishes

From Manchuria, small groups of armed fighters occasionally sneaked into the northern provinces, attacking Japanese police stations or cutting off supply lines. The Japanese responded with more garrisons, harsh crackdowns on border villages, and infiltration of the exile networks. This back-and-forth struggle shaped a mindset of resilience among northern Koreans who saw themselves as a frontline against the colonizers.

9.8 Cultural Nationalism: Arts, Media, and the Korean Language

Not all resistance was military or political. Many Koreans fought Japan's cultural assimilation by preserving and promoting the Korean language, literature, and arts.

9.8.1 Korean Language Societies

In the 1920s and 1930s, groups like the Korean Language Society tried to standardize Hangul spellings, publish dictionaries, and produce reading materials in Korean. While these societies were monitored by the police, they kept working in quiet.

- **Secret Classes**: Teachers in remote northern villages secretly held Hangul lessons, telling students never to mention these lessons outside.

9.8.2 Music and Drama

Traditional Korean music, pansori storytelling, and folk dances became tools for expressing hidden patriotism. Performers would weave subtle references to past Korean heroes into songs, lifting people's spirits. Even in the north's industrial towns, traveling performers could draw crowds hungry for a taste of their own culture.

9.8.3 Newspapers and Magazines

Some Korean-language newspapers were allowed after 1919, though heavily censored. They ran articles on modern science or global news but also slipped in pieces about Korean history and heroes. These stories reminded readers that their heritage was rich and unique. Many reading groups formed, especially in Christian churches or among students, to discuss such articles.

By protecting language, arts, and literature, these cultural nationalists helped ensure Korean identity would endure, even if direct political resistance was difficult.

9.9 The Shift Toward More Radical Resistance

As the 1930s progressed, Japan's policies became stricter again, demanding more of Korea's resources for war with China. The "cultural policy" softened, and assimilation efforts hardened. Sensing that peaceful paths were blocked, more Koreans turned to bolder methods.

9.9.1 Underground Militants

Some activists joined small militant cells that planned sabotage. They targeted police stations, pro-Japanese officials, or railway lines. Though these acts were dangerous, they showed that many Koreans had given up on moderate methods.

9.9.2 Links to Chinese Forces

Because Japan was now in open conflict with China, some Chinese nationalist or communist groups welcomed Korean fighters as allies. They provided training, weapons, or safe houses in Manchuria. These ties grew stronger after Japan intensified its campaign in northern China, leading to frequent skirmishes near the Korean-Manchurian border.

9.9.3 Harsh Punishments

Whenever the Japanese caught these militants, they responded with brutal punishments—public executions, torture, and collective fines on villages. Fear spread, but also anger. Many innocent farmers or miners were caught in the middle, fueling resentment that would not be forgotten.

9.10 Women's Expanded Role in Organized Resistance

Earlier, we noted how women got involved in the independence struggle. By the 1930s and early 1940s, many female activists took on even more responsibilities.

- **Training as Nurses or Aides**: Some joined guerrilla units, serving as medics or couriers.
- **Propaganda Writers**: Women who were literate composed pamphlets that called for an end to colonial rule.
- **Underground Leadership**: A few rose to leadership ranks in communist or nationalist cells, guiding younger recruits in sabotage missions or protests.

Though overshadowed by male figures in many historical accounts, these women were crucial in keeping the independence movement alive.

9.11 The Late Colonial Period: Wartime Mobilization

From the late 1930s onward, Japan was focused on its wars in China and the Pacific. Korea was forced to give more resources and manpower. This had a big impact on northern regions, where industrial and mining projects expanded rapidly.

9.11.1 Forced Labor and Military Draft

- **Factory Quotas**: Korean workers were made to fill quotas in factories that produced goods for the Japanese military.
- **Mining Expansion**: Mines in the north worked day and night to supply coal, iron, and other materials. Laborers faced dangerous conditions with no way to protest.
- **Military Conscription**: Toward the end of the war, Korean men were drafted into the Japanese army or navy. They had little choice but to obey, although some tried to flee across borders.

9.11.2 Intensified Cultural Suppression

During wartime, Japan demanded that Koreans prove their loyalty. This meant adopting Japanese names, worshiping at Shinto shrines, and speaking Japanese at all times. Schools that taught Hangul were under pressure to close or shift to a fully Japanese curriculum. Christian and other non-Shinto practices were frowned upon or shut down, though some continued in secret.

9.11.3 Underground Militancy Grows

Many activists saw Japan's overreach as a sign the empire might collapse if it lost the war. They increased sabotage acts against railway lines used for military transport, hoping to slow down Japanese war supplies. However, the Japanese cracked down viciously, using mass arrests and collective punishment.

9.12 International Support and the Korean Provisional Government

Outside Korea, notable figures had set up the Korean Provisional Government (KPG) in Shanghai in 1919. While it struggled to gain wide support or recognition, it served as a symbol of a "free Korea" in exile. Some of its members later moved to other parts of China, or even to the United States, to gather funds and diplomatic backing.

9.12.1 Limited Influence

The KPG did not directly control events inside Korea. Nevertheless, it kept the dream of independence visible on the world stage. It sent delegates to international meetings, wrote letters to foreign leaders, and spread propaganda about Japanese abuses.

9.12.2 Connections to Northern Activists

A few northern activists traveling through Manchuria or the Soviet Union made contact with the KPG. They shared intelligence about the situation at home. Though ideological differences sometimes appeared—some KPG members were moderate nationalists, while many northern fighters leaned socialist—both sides agreed on the end goal: a free Korea.

9.12.3 Global Awareness

As World War II raged, the Allies began discussing the future of territories occupied by Japan. Koreans hoped the Provisional Government or other resistance forces could convince the Allies to support an independent Korea once the war ended. This hope fueled continued resistance, even as conditions at home grew harsher.

9.13 Religious Groups and the Independence Spirit

Besides Christian and Buddhist communities, smaller religious or spiritual groups also contributed to the nationalist spirit. Donghak (Eastern Learning) and its successor movement, Cheondogyo, taught that all people were equal children of heaven. This idea empowered followers to resist any colonial authority that treated them as second-class citizens.

- **Cheondogyo Schools**: Some Cheondogyo believers opened private schools in northern towns, teaching moral lessons and Korean history.
- **Shared Networks**: They sometimes collaborated with Christians or local scholars, forming a broad alliance that supported independence behind the scenes.

Such alliances showed that, despite differences in doctrine, religious groups could unite over the shared purpose of Korean freedom.

9.14 Cultural Expression as Resistance

While direct confrontation was dangerous, cultural expression offered a less obvious path to unity. As assimilation tightened, more Koreans turned to subtle ways of defending their heritage.

9.14.1 Theater, Music, and Poetry

- **Plays**: Local theater groups performed historical dramas that hinted at Korea's struggles without naming Japan. Audiences understood the hidden message.

- **Music**: Folk songs praising farmland or ancient heroes reminded people of their roots.
- **Poetry**: Some poems written in Korean used natural scenery or old legends as symbols of resilience.

9.14.2 Private "Salon" Gatherings

In bigger northern towns, educated Koreans sometimes held "salon" gatherings in homes. They discussed literature, art, and classical Korean texts under the guise of social entertainment. These small circles helped keep the intellectual spirit of the resistance alive.

9.15 The Final Phase of Colonial Rule

By 1944 and 1945, Japan's defeat in World War II seemed likely. Allied forces pressed closer, and supply lines to the Japanese mainland were stretched. In Korea, the colonial government became even more desperate to meet resource needs.

9.15.1 Increased Forced Labor

Many Koreans were forced to move to Japan itself to work in war factories. Others were sent to territories Japan still held in China or Southeast Asia. This mass uprooting caused heartbreak and separation for countless families.

9.15.2 Heightened Surveillance

Japanese police monitored every movement of suspected nationalists or communists. They raided homes, shut down schools, and arrested anyone who owned banned books. Informers were paid to keep watch on neighbors.

9.15.3 Hope from Abroad

Despite this dark atmosphere, rumors spread that Allied powers had promised to free Korea once Japan was defeated. Underground groups braced for a final chance to rise. Some activists made contact with Soviet or Chinese forces near the border, preparing to coordinate actions when war ended.

9.16 Liberation in Sight

In August 1945, Japan surrendered following the atomic bombs on Hiroshima and Nagasaki and the Soviet declaration of war against Japan in Manchuria. Suddenly, after decades of harsh rule, Korea's colonial master was gone.

- **Emotional Reactions**: People poured onto the streets, tearing down Japanese signs and flags, singing Korean anthems, and flying homemade Korean flags (the Taegukgi).
- **Power Vacuum**: There was no central Korean authority ready to take over immediately. Political groups tried to form local committees, hoping to manage order until a national government could be established.

- **Northern Dynamics**: In the north, Soviets moved in fast from across the Manchurian border, while American forces would later arrive in the south. This set the stage for the peninsula's division.

9.17 Lasting Impact of Resistance Movements

Although Korean independence came more from Japan's broader defeat in World War II than from a single uprising, the long years of resistance were not in vain. They kept alive the Korean sense of unity and dignity under brutal suppression. They produced leaders who understood the importance of standing firm for their country's future.

- **Political Ideologies**: Over decades, activists had formed different ideological stances. Some were nationalists with moderate views, others were socialists or communists. These distinctions would soon matter greatly in post-liberation politics, especially in the north.
- **Social Changes**: Years of underground activism also meant women and lower-class workers had gained experience in organizing and leadership. This paved the way for deeper social changes in the new era.
- **Regional Identity**: Northern fighters, in particular, felt proud of their local efforts, crossing into Manchuria and teaming up with anti-Japanese guerrillas. That pride would become part of the narrative for the leadership that emerged in the north after 1945.

CHAPTER 10

THE END OF WORLD WAR II AND THE DIVISION OF KOREA

Introduction

For 35 years, Korea was under Japanese colonial rule, enduring forced cultural assimilation, hard labor, and the suppression of independence movements. By the mid-1940s, Japan's imperial ambitions were crumbling in the face of Allied advances during World War II. Finally, in August 1945, Japan surrendered. This was a joyous moment for Koreans, who celebrated liberation from colonial oppression. But the celebration quickly turned to uncertainty. Who would govern Korea now that Japanese power had vanished?

In this chapter, we examine the chaotic events that followed Japan's defeat, focusing on how foreign powers—mainly the Soviet Union in the north and the United States in the south—arrived to fill the power vacuum. We see how local committees tried to take charge, why the Allied powers decided to split the peninsula, and how tensions rose between different Korean political groups. This period, from 1945 to the late 1940s, led directly to the permanent division of Korea. While the modern-day results of that division go beyond this book's historical scope, understanding these first steps is crucial for seeing how North Korea (the DPRK) eventually formed its own distinct state.

10.1 Liberation Day: August 15, 1945

After two atomic bombs on Hiroshima and Nagasaki, plus the Soviet entry into the war against Japan, the Japanese government announced its surrender on August 15, 1945. In Korea, that date is remembered as **Gwangbokjeol** or "Restoration of Light."

10.1.1 Public Joy

Across the peninsula, people rushed into the streets. They tore down Japanese signs, burned symbols of colonial rule, and raised the Korean flag. Factories and schools stopped following Japanese orders. Farmers halted grain shipments intended for Japanese soldiers.

10.1.2 Collapse of Authority

Japanese police and officials, who had once held absolute power, suddenly lost their authority. Some fled or tried to hide, fearing retaliation. Others destroyed documents to cover up their past actions. This left a vacuum at every level of governance—there was no functioning Korean government ready to step in.

10.1.3 Local Committees Form

Ordinary Koreans, including former activists, students, and religious leaders, formed "People's Committees" to maintain order and organize public services. In some towns, these committees acted like temporary governments. They set rules for markets, tried to prevent looting, and dealt with local disputes. Many activists who had led resistance groups saw this as their chance to shape a new Korea.

10.2 Arrival of Soviet Forces in the North

While Koreans celebrated, Soviet troops were moving into Manchuria, defeating Japanese units there. They quickly crossed into northern Korea, aiming to disarm remaining Japanese forces.

10.2.1 Crossing the Border

On August 8, 1945, the Soviet Union declared war on Japan. Within days, the Red Army entered Korea through the north. By the end of the month, Soviet soldiers occupied key northern cities, including Pyongyang and Hamhung.

10.2.2 First Impressions

For Koreans in the north, the Soviets were both liberators (removing the Japanese) and foreign strangers. Some Koreans welcomed them with relief, hoping the Soviets would support full independence. Others worried about what Soviet influence might bring, recalling that communist ideas had circulated among some resistance fighters.

10.2.3 Disarming the Japanese

The main Soviet mission was to disarm the Japanese army and ensure no new threat to Soviet territory. Soviet officers replaced Japanese administrators in government offices. However, they needed local Korean help to run day-to-day affairs, so they often recognized or cooperated with existing People's Committees if those committees seemed friendly to communist or left-leaning policies.

10.3 The American Occupation in the South

On September 8, 1945, U.S. forces arrived in the southern port of Incheon. Their official task was similar: accept the Japanese surrender and maintain order until a stable government could be formed.

10.3.1 The 38th Parallel

Before the Americans landed, the U.S. and Soviet governments hastily agreed on a temporary dividing line for their respective occupations. They chose the **38th Parallel**—a line of latitude cutting roughly across the middle of the peninsula. Soviet troops would oversee disarmament north of that line, while Americans would do the same in the south.

10.3.2 Reinstating Old Systems

Unlike the Soviets, who often recognized local Korean committees, the Americans were more skeptical of grassroots groups (many of which had leftist leanings). The U.S. military government sometimes kept Japanese or pro-Japanese Korean officials in their posts, at least temporarily, believing it was necessary to restore order. This angered many Korean nationalists who had fought against Japanese rule.

10.3.3 Confusion and Resentment

While some Koreans welcomed American soldiers, others felt disappointed that the south was not allowed to govern itself. People in the south, hearing news of how the Soviets had recognized local committees in the north, wondered why the U.S. authorities did not do the same. Tensions began to build between conservative and leftist groups, each blaming the other for the slow pace of establishing a national government.

10.4 The People's Committees and Political Divisions

In the months right after liberation, Koreans all over the peninsula formed People's Committees or local councils. These groups often included members of various ideologies: nationalists, communists, Christians, and more. But differences soon emerged.

10.4.1 Northern People's Committees

In the north, many committees had strong socialist or communist leadership. This made it easier for them to align with the Soviet forces. They declared goals like land reform, workers' rights, and removing all traces of Japanese-era landlords or collaborators.

10.4.2 Southern People's Committees

Similar committees appeared in the south, but the U.S. military government distrusted them, suspecting communist influence. American officers sometimes dissolved these committees, clashed with them, or replaced their members with conservative figures who had not fought against Japan as strongly but were seen as reliable or anti-communist.

10.4.3 Ideological Rifts

By late 1945, it was clear the peninsula was splitting into two broad political camps:

- **Leftist/Communist Camp**: Strong in the north, it gained support from Soviet backing and from peasants who wanted radical change.
- **Conservative/Right-Wing Camp**: More influential in the south, supported by American authorities and many wealthy landowners who feared communist takeovers.

These rifts set the stage for further clashes over Korea's future.

10.5 International Debates on Korea's Future

While Koreans on the ground grappled with new realities, the global powers met at international conferences to discuss the fate of Asia. The question was: **Should Korea become independent right away, or undergo a period of trusteeship** under foreign guidance?

10.5.1 The Moscow Conference (December 1945)

At the Moscow Conference, the U.S., the Soviet Union, and Britain agreed (at least on paper) that Korea would eventually become free. However, they also suggested a **five-year trusteeship** to help Korea rebuild. This idea angered many Koreans, who felt they had already endured too much foreign rule.

- **Northern Reaction**: Some communist leaders in the north initially opposed trusteeship too, but when the Soviet Union endorsed it, they adjusted their stance to match Moscow's line.
- **Southern Reaction**: In the south, people held large protests against trusteeship, calling it another form of occupation.

10.5.2 Joint Commission Meetings

Between 1946 and 1947, a Joint Commission of Soviet and U.S. representatives met to figure out how to form a unified Korean government. But they disagreed on which Korean groups should be allowed to participate. The Soviets insisted that leftist groups be included, while the Americans blocked those suspected of communist ties. Meetings ended in stalemate, increasing distrust on both sides.

10.6 Developments in the North: Early Reforms

While global talks stalled, local authorities in the north pressed on with reforms under Soviet guidance. These actions laid the foundation for what would become the Democratic People's Republic of Korea (North Korea).

10.6.1 Land Reform

One of the biggest changes was **land reform**. Large estates owned by Japanese nationals or pro-Japanese Korean landlords were confiscated. Land was then redistributed to poor farmers. This move was very popular among peasants, who had suffered under high rents during the colonial era.

10.6.2 Nationalization of Industry

Factories and mines that had belonged to Japanese companies were nationalized. The new administration said these resources should belong to the people. Many workers saw this as a positive change, believing it would end exploitation. Soviet advisors helped organize production and management.

10.6.3 Emergence of Local Leaders

Some of the key figures in the northern administration were individuals with a background in anti-Japanese guerrilla fighting, often linked to the Soviet Union or communist networks. They claimed legitimacy through their resistance credentials. For many northerners, these leaders seemed like true patriots, finally throwing off colonial-era injustices.

Though not yet called "North Korea," the area above the 38th Parallel was clearly moving in a different direction from the south.

10.7 Developments in the South: Conservative Government

In the south, the American Military Government faced the tricky task of restoring order while avoiding a communist takeover. They often worked with established Korean conservatives who had property and influence.

10.7.1 Continued Influence of Former Collaborators

Because many skilled administrators under Japanese rule were the only ones with bureaucratic experience, the Americans kept some in office. This angered independence activists who felt these people were tainted by their past collaboration with the colonial government.

10.7.2 Formation of Right-Wing Parties

New political parties emerged, often led by exiled nationalists who had returned from abroad. The most famous of these was led by Syngman Rhee, a long-time independence activist educated in the United States. He gained American support by promoting a staunch anti-communist stance.

10.7.3 Public Unrest

Large segments of the southern population remained poor, jobless, and frustrated. Strikes by workers and uprisings by peasants demanding land reform were often suppressed by the police or military forces, now overseen by the U.S. occupation. This fueled resentment and occasional clashes between leftists and conservatives.

10.8 The Role of Kim Il Sung in the North

Among the former guerrilla fighters welcomed by Soviet authorities in the north was **Kim Il Sung**. He had fought against the Japanese in Manchuria and the Soviet Far East. In late 1945, the Soviets introduced him to the people of Pyongyang as a hero of the anti-Japanese struggle.

10.8.1 Rising Political Influence

Kim Il Sung took key positions within the local communist party structure. He gave speeches promising to build a new society free from landlords and colonial exploiters. Backed by Soviet advisors, his influence grew rapidly.

10.8.2 Uniting Various Groups

At that time, the north's communist party included different factions—some aligned more with domestic activists, others with Chinese communist ties. Kim Il Sung, with Soviet support, gradually outmaneuvered rivals. By the late 1940s, he was clearly in control of the main leadership circle.

10.8.3 Popularity Among Peasants

The land reform and nationalization policies, combined with Kim Il Sung's image as a guerrilla hero, made him popular among many northern peasants and workers. Though behind the scenes there were intense power struggles, the public saw him as the face of a new, independent north.

10.9 Increasing Tensions Along the 38th Parallel

As both sides developed separate administrative systems, the dividing line at the 38th Parallel hardened. Families living near the boundary sometimes found themselves split, with relatives on opposite sides.

10.9.1 Border Incidents

Small border incidents flared up. Armed units from each side occasionally skirmished, accusing the other of trespassing or harboring spies. Civilians crossing the line to visit relatives risked arrest.

10.9.2 Propaganda Wars

Both sides used propaganda, accusing each other of betraying Korean unity. In the north, newspapers claimed that southern elites were puppets of American imperialism. In the south, leaders warned that northern officials were mere tools of Soviet communism. Ordinary people, weary from decades of colonial rule, were caught in the middle of this political rivalry.

10.10 Attempts at a Unified Government Fail

Between 1946 and 1947, various committees and representatives from the north and south tried to organize a single national assembly or some form of unified authority. But ideological conflicts and foreign interference blocked every effort.

- **Right-Left Coalition**: There were fleeting attempts by moderate leaders to bridge the gap, but extremists on both sides fought these compromises.
- **U.N. Involvement**: By late 1947, the United Nations took up the "Korean question," proposing elections under U.N. supervision. The Soviets refused to allow U.N. officials into the north, claiming it was a violation of their sphere of influence.

Without agreement, the stage was set for separate elections in the south only, leading to a divided system.

10.11 Formation of the Republic of Korea (South)

In May 1948, the south held elections under U.N. oversight, though not all parties participated. Syngman Rhee's allies won, and on August 15, 1948, the **Republic of Korea** (ROK) was officially declared in Seoul. Rhee became the first president.

10.11.1 Reaction in the North

Northern leaders denounced these elections as illegal, stating that the south had betrayed national unity. They quickly prepared for their own separate government.

10.11.2 Withdrawal of U.S. Forces

After the Republic of Korea formed, most American occupation troops began to leave, though some advisors stayed. This shift gave the south a sense of formal independence, but it also meant fewer American troops on the ground to deter any military clash with the north.

10.12 Formation of the Democratic People's Republic of Korea (North)

Encouraged by the Soviets, northern authorities convened their own assembly in Pyongyang. On September 9, 1948, they announced the founding of the **Democratic People's Republic of Korea** (DPRK), with Kim Il Sung as the Premier.

10.12.1 Soviet Endorsement

The Soviet Union recognized the new DPRK government almost immediately. Kim Il Sung publicly promised to unify the peninsula under his government, claiming the south's leadership was illegitimate.

10.12.2 Consolidation of Power

In the following months, Kim Il Sung's regime moved to eliminate or sideline any rival voices. Some non-communist or moderate leftist figures were pushed out of the leadership. The DPRK adopted policies that mirrored Soviet-style socialism, emphasizing state ownership and centralized planning.

10.12.3 Social Support

Many in the north supported the new government wholeheartedly because of land reform successes and the promise of building a strong independent state. At the same time, anyone critical of the new regime risked being labeled an enemy.

10.13 Deepening Division and the 38th Parallel's Solidification

By late 1948, two separate Korean governments each claimed to be the only legitimate authority for the entire peninsula. The dividing line at the 38th Parallel became a de facto international boundary.

- **Border Tensions**: Small-scale fighting occasionally flared along the boundary, with each side accusing the other of provocations.
- **Population Movements**: Some people fled south, fearing communist policies. Others went north, attracted by land reform or leftist ideals.
- **Family Splits**: Families that had members in both regions had almost no safe way to reunite.

What began as a temporary military occupation line in 1945 was now a dividing border between two governments with starkly different ideologies.

10.14 The Role of Foreign Powers

The U.S. and the Soviet Union set the parameters for Korea's division. Both had broader global concerns, as the Cold War was taking shape.

10.14.1 Soviet Goals

The Soviets saw the north as a strategic buffer zone against any future threats from Japan or the U.S. They provided military training and equipment to the new DPRK army.

10.14.2 American Goals

The Americans, worried about communism's spread in Asia, backed the southern government, hoping to build a stable, anti-communist ally in the region.

10.14.3 Cold War Context

Korea soon became a frontline in the broader Cold War struggle. Each superpower wanted to ensure its influence over its respective Korean partner. This tug-of-war overshadowed Korean desires for a single, independent state.

10.15 Economic and Social Paths Diverge

From 1948 onward, the north and south started forging different economic and social paths:

1. **North (DPRK):**

    - Rapid nationalization of all industries.

    - Collective or state-owned farming.

    - A single-party system led by Kim Il Sung, with close Soviet ties.

2. **South (ROK):**

    - Mixed economy, with both private ownership and some state intervention.

- Initial reliance on U.S. aid for rebuilding.

- Multi-party elections on paper, though Syngman Rhee's government often suppressed opposition.

These contrasting models hardened the notion that one Korea was turning socialist, the other capitalist.

10.16 Growing Military Strength on Both Sides

As the 1940s ended, both the DPRK and the ROK built up their armed forces. Training and weapon supplies came from their respective allies.

- **Northern Forces**: Many officers were veterans of anti-Japanese guerrilla fighting or had trained in the Soviet Union. They were shaped into a formal army with modern equipment from Soviet arsenals.
- **Southern Forces**: The U.S. helped form a national police force and later a small army. Training was rushed, but it gave the ROK some capacity to control uprisings or border incidents.

Tensions rose, with each side suspecting that the other might try to unify Korea by force. This distrust would soon have tragic results.

10.17 Public Sentiment in the North

For many ordinary northerners, the end of Japanese rule and the birth of the DPRK seemed like a chance for a fresh start. Landless peasants received farmland, while factory workers gained a sense of pride in "people's ownership." Schools taught Korean language without Japanese interference, and references to old independence fighters were openly celebrated.

However, life was not perfect. Some people feared the new communist-style system, especially those who had owned property. Others worried about forced political conformity. Yet, in the spirit of liberation, a majority appeared to support the new direction, at least in the early phase.

10.18 Immediate Consequences of Division

By 1949 and 1950, the division was firmly set. Communication between north and south was almost impossible. Families remained split, trade routes were cut off, and each side had a separate currency and bureaucracy.

- **Diplomatic Recognition**: The DPRK was recognized by socialist bloc countries like the Soviet Union and China. The ROK was recognized by the U.S. and other Western nations.
- **Propaganda**: Both governments claimed to be the true voice of the Korean people. Radios and newspapers in each zone demonized the other side.
- **Clashes**: Skirmishes along the 38th Parallel grew more frequent, with casualties on both sides. The stage was set for a larger conflict that would break out in mid-1950.

10.20 Conclusion

World War II's end brought Korea its long-awaited liberation from Japan, but it did not bring lasting peace or unity. The sudden collapse of Japanese authority, along with the entry of Soviet and American troops, led to a deep rift. Northern leaders shaped a socialist system under Kim Il Sung and Soviet influence, while southern leaders established a separate republic aligned with the United States.

In just a few short years, the peninsula was split into two political entities, each refusing to acknowledge the other's legitimacy. Families and communities divided at the 38th Parallel faced a stark new reality. Hopes for a unified Korea faded as the Cold War turned the peninsula into a geopolitical battleground. The following chapters will explore how the north continued to develop, guided by Kim Il Sung's rule and shaped by the ideology of self-reliance, known as **Juche**. But for now, we conclude our look at how Korea went from liberation to division—a crucial turning point in the formation of what we later call **North Korea**.

CHAPTER 11

THE BIRTH OF NORTH KOREA (DPRK)

Introduction

By the late 1940s, Korea stood divided along the 38th Parallel. In the north, a new government was rapidly taking shape under Soviet guidance. Reforms such as land redistribution and factory nationalization won support from peasants and workers, while people began to see emerging leaders like Kim Il Sung as symbols of a fresh start. On September 9, 1948, the Democratic People's Republic of Korea (DPRK) was officially proclaimed, marking the beginning of a separate northern state.

In this chapter, we will explore the formation of the DPRK, looking at the social, economic, and political shifts that occurred in the north after World War II. We will see how Soviet advisors helped set up new structures, how local leaders rose to prominence, and what life was like for everyday people caught in a time of massive transition. Though many welcomed these changes, others worried about the communist style of government or missed family members now living in the south. This chapter gives us a deeper look into how the state of North Korea emerged from the chaos and hope of post-liberation Korea.

11.1 A Climate of Change and Urgency

The end of Japanese rule in 1945 brought sudden freedom to Korea, but also tremendous uncertainty. Factories and government offices were left without direction. The Soviets, arriving in the north, had to establish order quickly. Their top priority was disarming Japanese troops and ensuring no revived threat to Soviet interests.

At the same time, northern activists and political groups formed local People's Committees. These committees had begun as grassroots organizations, taking over basic functions like policing, rationing food, and keeping schools running. Now, under Soviet oversight, the committees expanded, sometimes merging or reorganizing into larger administrative bodies. Many committee members were aligned with leftist or communist ideals, though some nationalists and religious figures also participated.

11.1.1 Urgency to Rebuild

Workers and peasants had endured harsh Japanese policies for decades. Mines, roads, and railways in the north were worn out or damaged. Farmland needed repairs, especially after many years of forced production to feed Japan's war effort. With the Soviets encouraging quick reforms, local leaders seized the moment. They believed that by rapidly restructuring land ownership and industry, they could erase old injustices.

11.1.2 Support from Soviet Advisors

Soviet military officials and civilian advisors guided this transformation, but they also allowed Koreans to take a leading role, at least in public. They brought in translators and set up short training courses for local administrators, teaching them how to run a centralized, planned economy. The Soviets delivered supplies, such as grain and machinery, to stabilize the region, hoping to gain goodwill among northerners.

11.2 Establishing New Political Structures

Even before declaring itself a separate country, the north had begun creating formal governing bodies. These would later evolve into the cabinet ministries, local assemblies, and mass organizations of the DPRK.

11.2.1 People's Committees Evolve

Immediately after liberation, People's Committees sprang up in almost every town and county. By 1946, these committees were reorganized into a more unified system under a central body known as the North Korean Provisional People's Committee. This group, chaired by Kim Il Sung, enacted important policies such as land reform.

- **Local Authority**: In villages, smaller committees handled disputes, distributed land, and organized community projects. They reported upward to county-level committees, which in turn reported to provincial and central authorities in Pyongyang.
- **Consolidation**: Over time, differing political voices were either absorbed into or replaced by communist-dominated structures. Non-communist or moderate socialists found themselves sidelined if they did not follow the new line set by Kim Il Sung's circle.

11.2.2 Formation of a Central Government

Throughout 1947 and early 1948, the northern administration drafted frameworks for a constitution and national institutions. By late 1948, they were ready to declare a full-fledged state:

1. **Constitution**: A new constitution promised rights to workers, peasants, and women, and pledged to build a socialist society free from exploitation.
2. **Cabinet**: Ministries for defense, finance, education, and more were formed. Many leading positions went to individuals with proven loyalty to Kim Il Sung or who had close ties to Soviet authorities.
3. **Mass Organizations**: Groups for youth, women, and workers were set up to involve ordinary citizens in political life and to spread propaganda about the government's goals.

This structure aimed to centralize power around Kim Il Sung and his allies, with guidance from Soviet advisors. While it boasted about popular participation, real decisions often came from the top.

11.3 Land Reform: Transforming Rural Society

One of the first and most significant acts of the new northern government was **land reform**. Under Japanese colonialism, large estates dominated farming, and many peasants worked as tenant farmers, paying high rents. Post-liberation leadership saw land reform as crucial to winning the support of rural populations.

11.3.1 Key Steps of Land Reform

- **Confiscation of Japanese Land**: All land previously owned by Japanese nationals or the colonial government was seized.
- **Expropriation of Collaborators**: Koreans accused of collaborating with Japanese authorities could also lose their property.
- **Redistribution**: The seized land was divided into smaller plots and given to landless or poor peasants. Families that had previously rented land found themselves owning it, often for the first time.

11.3.2 Impact on Peasant Life

For many rural families, this was a dream come true. They could finally farm their own fields without paying crushing rent. Scenes of joy were common, with peasants gathering to celebrate the new policies. The government often organized meetings in village squares, where local officials read aloud the names of people receiving land. This policy caused a surge in support for the new northern authorities.

At the same time, landowners—especially those seen as pro-Japanese—lost nearly everything. Some fled south to avoid repercussions. Others tried to appeal, but few succeeded. This shift greatly reduced the old landlord class in the north, paving the way for a more equal, though still state-controlled, agrarian society.

11.3.3 Hidden Challenges

While popular among peasants, land reform also led to confusion at times. Surveying fields accurately was not easy. Some disputes over boundaries popped up, causing local committees to hold lengthy hearings. Nevertheless, the overall outcome was a major boost for the new government's popularity in villages across the north.

11.4 Nationalization of Industry

In parallel with land reform, the north's administration also nationalized key industries. Under Japanese rule, large companies had controlled mines, railways, and factories. Many of these were abandoned when the Japanese left, so the new government argued these assets should belong to the people.

11.4.1 The Process

- **Takeover of Japanese Assets**: Factories and mines left behind were declared state property.
- **Management Structures**: Soviet-style management boards were set up in each facility, often headed by a Korean official who took directives from Pyongyang.
- **Workers' Committees**: Within each factory, workers formed committees to oversee day-to-day production. These committees were expected to enforce safety, track output, and promote socialist values, though they still answered to higher authorities.

11.4.2 Effects on Workers

For many industrial workers, this was a dramatic change. Instead of working for Japanese owners, they now officially worked "for the state." Wages remained modest, but new slogans claimed that workers were building a society for themselves. The government introduced literacy programs in some workplaces, aiming to educate and politically motivate employees.

However, the sudden shift in ownership did not solve all problems. Machinery was often outdated, and technical experts were in short supply, as many Japanese managers had departed. Soviet advisors tried to fill the gap, training local engineers or bringing in some Soviet specialists. Nonetheless, many factories struggled with frequent breakdowns and a lack of spare parts.

11.5 Kim Il Sung's Growing Influence

While several political figures had been active in northern politics, Kim Il Sung quickly rose to a leading position. This was not purely accidental. The Soviets believed Kim's background in anti-Japanese guerrilla warfare, combined with his loyalty to Moscow, made him a suitable figurehead.

11.5.1 Cultivating an Image

In public speeches, Kim Il Sung was portrayed as the valiant fighter who battled the Japanese in Manchuria. Newspapers and radio broadcasts told stories of his bravery, though details were often exaggerated or lacking evidence. This image appealed to northerners who wanted heroes to admire after years of oppression.

11.5.2 Dealing with Rivals

Other communists or nationalists had also resisted Japan, but those who did not align with Kim's approach or who had strong independent power bases were gradually removed from high office. Some were labeled "spies" or "reactionaries," forcing them to leave politics or flee. This consolidation ensured that Kim faced limited internal opposition as he shaped the north's new state.

11.5.3 Support from Ordinary People

For many workers and peasants, Kim Il Sung's leadership seemed beneficial. Land reform, industrial nationalization, and mass education efforts all signaled positive change. Northern propaganda channels credited these improvements to Kim's wisdom and leadership, further boosting his popularity.

11.6 Everyday Life in the Emerging DPRK

Between 1945 and 1948, everyday life in the north transformed at a startling pace. Some changes were met with excitement, while others brought worries and confusion.

11.6.1 Education and Literacy

The new administration launched campaigns to improve literacy rates. Teachers, often volunteers or party members, visited villages and taught Hangul to adults who had grown up under Japanese rule. Schools reopened with a Korean-based curriculum, removing Japanese language texts.

- **Political Themes**: Classes included lessons on socialism, national pride, and the achievements of the "people's government." While such lessons aimed to inspire, they also introduced early signs of indoctrination.

11.6.2 Food and Housing

Peasants who received land initially saw better food security. However, distribution of supplies was sometimes uneven, especially in mountainous areas. The government began discussing plans for future cooperative farms, but at this early stage, many families still farmed their newly allocated plots on their own. In cities, housing shortages were common due to rapid urban migration. Vacant Japanese-owned properties were turned into communal housing or offices, though conditions could be cramped.

11.6.3 Social Organizations

Mass organizations for women, youth, and workers sprang up everywhere, holding meetings to discuss local issues and plan communal events. Membership was strongly encouraged, and these groups helped the government spread information quickly. They also served as ways to keep track of the population, a hint that surveillance measures would become more rigorous over time.

11.7 The September 9, 1948 Proclamation

By mid-1948, two separate governments existed on the peninsula. The south had formed the Republic of Korea in August. In response, the north convened its own Supreme People's Assembly, ratified a new constitution, and on September 9, declared itself the Democratic People's Republic of Korea (DPRK), with Kim Il Sung as its Premier.

11.7.1 The Official Ceremony

In Pyongyang, crowds gathered to witness the ceremony. Speeches proclaimed the dawn of a people's state that would unite all Koreans under socialism. The new flag of the DPRK was raised, and messages of congratulation came from the Soviet Union and other socialist-leaning countries.

11.7.2 International Recognition

Almost immediately, the Soviet Union recognized the DPRK as the legitimate government of Korea. Countries aligned with the socialist bloc followed suit. Meanwhile, Western countries, led by the United States, recognized the Republic of Korea (ROK) in the south. This deepened the peninsula's division, making it part of the larger global tension known as the Cold War.

11.7.3 Promises to Reunify

In official statements, DPRK leaders insisted they would reunify Korea under their system. Propaganda portrayed the southern government as a puppet of American imperialism. People in the north were told it was only a matter of time before the southern masses rose up to join the DPRK's socialist cause.

11.8 Political Parties and the One-Party Dominance

Though the new constitution allowed multiple political parties in name, the reality was that the Workers' Party of Korea (WPK)—formed from a merger of smaller socialist and communist groups—dominated public life.

- **Workers' Party of Korea**: Kim Il Sung led the northern branch of this party. Through organizational discipline and control of security forces, the WPK set policy.
- **Minor Parties**: There were minor parties, like the Chondoist Chongu Party (linked to the Cheondogyo religious movement) and the Korean Social Democratic Party. However, they functioned under WPK leadership, supporting its policies in practice.
- **Political Conformity**: Over time, any voice that disagreed with the WPK's official line risked being labeled a traitor. Fear of being denounced led most officials and citizens to show loyalty, or at least pretend loyalty.

Thus, while the constitution mentioned democratic rights, in reality the system was quickly converging toward one-party rule.

11.9 Military Organization and Soviets' Role

A key pillar of the emerging DPRK was the creation of a strong military. Former guerrillas and new recruits formed the Korean People's Army (KPA). The Soviet Union supplied weapons and training, seeing the KPA as a buffer against any attacks from the south.

11.9.1 Building the KPA

- **Guerrilla Veterans**: Many high-ranking officers had fought alongside Kim Il Sung in anti-Japanese units.
- **Soviet Instructors**: Soviet military advisors taught modern tactics, how to use tanks, artillery, and aircraft.
- **Rapid Growth**: By 1949, the KPA had tens of thousands of soldiers, well-armed compared to the relatively smaller force in the south.

11.9.2 Tensions at the Border

With each side building up its military, the 38th Parallel grew more tense. Skirmishes erupted frequently, raising fears of a larger conflict. DPRK propaganda told northerners that the south was illegally occupied by U.S. forces and that war might be needed to reunify the country.

11.10 Challenges and Opposition

Not everyone in the north welcomed the new order. Some groups or individuals had reservations about the rapid changes, especially if they were losing property or worried about communist policies.

11.10.1 Ex-Collaborators or Landlords

People labeled as pro-Japanese collaborators often faced public trials, social shaming, or worse. Some landlords had their land seized, leaving them with nothing. A number of them tried to flee south, sneaking across the border to avoid arrest or reprisals.

11.10.2 Religious Concerns

While the early DPRK constitution guaranteed religious freedom, many Christian churches felt uneasy. They noticed the government was promoting a socialist worldview that discouraged religious practices, seeing them as outdated. Some church leaders who spoke out faced harassment.

11.10.3 Intra-Party Rivalries

Within the communist ranks, there were factions: some members had ties to Chinese communists, others to Soviet communists, and still others were local activists. Kim Il Sung skillfully balanced these groups, but internal tensions sometimes flared. Over the next few years, Kim would move to remove or marginalize rival factions.

11.11 The Ideological Backbone: Early Juche Ideas

Though the formal Juche ideology (meaning "self-reliance") was not yet fully fleshed out, early hints of it appeared. Kim Il Sung and his circle stressed building a nation that relied on its own resources, free from external domination.

- **Korean-Style Socialism**: They claimed that while Soviet help was valued, the DPRK would chart its own path, based on Korea's specific conditions.
- **National Pride**: Propaganda highlighted the idea that Koreans had a proud history, and now, under the DPRK, they could become masters of their destiny.
- **Roots of Juche**: In speeches, Kim Il Sung mentioned independence and self-reliance in vague terms. Over time, these concepts would evolve into the official state ideology that shaped every aspect of life in North Korea.

For now, the focus was on practical tasks: reorganizing farmland, boosting production, and unifying the population under one political line.

11.12 Society Under Construction

Life in the newly proclaimed DPRK was a mix of hope, propaganda, and uncertainty. Everyone was urged to participate in building a socialist paradise. Neighborhood groups organized cleaning projects, literacy classes, and cultural events. The government encouraged stories of heroic farmers or workers who exceeded production targets, hoping to inspire others.

11.12.1 Changing Family Dynamics

Traditional Korean family structures began to shift. Women were encouraged to work in factories or take leadership roles in mass organizations, although in practice, many still handled household duties. The government passed laws promoting equality, such as banning arranged marriages and allowing for more liberal divorce rules.

11.12.2 Collective Spirit

The official media promoted the "collective spirit," praising neighbors who helped each other in communal farm work or city clean-ups. People were told to set aside personal interests for the good of society. Those who resisted or seemed too individualistic might face criticism sessions, where neighbors publicly questioned their loyalty to the socialist cause.

11.12.3 Art and Culture

Artists were encouraged to create works that celebrated the new era. Paintings showed happy peasants harvesting abundant crops, or factory workers with smiling faces. Traditional folk dances were adapted to include patriotic themes. Though such cultural activities were lively, they also hinted at growing state control over artistic expression.

11.13 The Outside World Looks On

Observers outside Korea watched these developments with mixed reactions:

- **Soviet Satisfaction**: The Soviet Union was generally pleased with the DPRK's moves, seeing it as a reliable ally on its eastern flank. Soviet newspapers ran stories praising Kim Il Sung's leadership.
- **Chinese Observations**: China had just concluded its own civil war by 1949 and was establishing the People's Republic of China. Some Chinese communists saw parallels and expected close ties with the DPRK.

- **Western Distrust**: Western nations, allied with the Republic of Korea in the south, viewed the DPRK's steps as expansion of communist influence in East Asia. American and European newspapers wrote of a "Soviet puppet state."

International tension rose as each side suspected the other of plotting to unify the peninsula under their preferred system.

11.14 Mounting Pressures Toward Conflict

By early 1950, both the DPRK and the Republic of Korea were heavily armed. Each claimed legitimate authority over the entire peninsula, refusing to recognize the other. Small border clashes escalated. Many historians note that by the spring of 1950, tensions were at a boiling point.

11.14.1 Kim Il Sung's Ambitions

According to various accounts, Kim Il Sung strongly believed the south would rise in support of northern forces if conflict broke out. He insisted that most southerners despised the Rhee government and would welcome liberation by the DPRK. Meanwhile, he sought approval from Stalin in the Soviet Union and later from Mao Zedong in China to unify Korea by military means.

11.14.2 Southern Determination

In the south, Syngman Rhee's regime also talked about unification by force, wanting to push north and end communism in Korea. The Cold War context emboldened both sides to think they had backing from powerful allies.

11.14.3 The Spark of War

As each side geared up, it seemed only a matter of time before open war would erupt. American and Soviet interests loomed large, setting the stage for a brutal conflict that would reshape the peninsula's future. Though the details of the Korean War belong in the next chapter, it is important to see how the birth of the DPRK and the separate southern government laid the foundation for this deadly confrontation.

11.15 Setting the Stage for the Future

By mid-1950, the DPRK had taken several defining steps:

1. **Official Formation (1948)**: A separate government recognized by socialist states.
2. **Land and Industry Reforms**: Gaining peasant and worker support by redistributing wealth, albeit under strong state control.
3. **Growing Personality Cult**: Kim Il Sung's image as a heroic liberator took root, though it was not yet as dominant as it would become in later decades.
4. **One-Party Dominance**: Alternative viewpoints were marginalized, preparing the way for a strongly centralized authority.

Though the DPRK was still young and faced huge challenges—technical shortfalls, limited resources, and potential hostility from the south—it had a sense of momentum. With Soviet backing and a loyal base of supporters in the countryside, the new leadership felt confident they could shape an independent socialist future.

CHAPTER 12

KIM IL SUNG'S EARLY LEADERSHIP

Introduction

By the end of 1948, Kim Il Sung stood at the helm of the Democratic People's Republic of Korea (DPRK). He was presented as the central hero of the nation's founding story—an anti-Japanese guerrilla fighter who would guide the north toward prosperity and eventual reunification. However, his path to power was neither simple nor uncontested. He had to consolidate authority over rival communist factions, navigate Soviet and Chinese influences, and prepare for the possibility of war with the south.

In this chapter, we will dig deeper into Kim Il Sung's early leadership. We will see how he managed internal politics, built a personality cult, and led sweeping reforms. We will also note how the looming Cold War tensions shaped his decisions, culminating in the start of the Korean War in 1950. This period defined the DPRK's trajectory and laid the groundwork for the Kim family's long rule over the north.

12.1 The Guerrilla Background: Fact or Legend?

A key factor in Kim Il Sung's rise was his reputation as a courageous guerrilla fighter against Japanese colonists. But how much of this story was fact, and how much was carefully constructed image?

12.1.1 Early Activities

Born as Kim Song-ju in 1912, he spent some of his youth in Manchuria, where he joined various anti-Japanese movements. He indeed participated in guerrilla warfare under communist groups, sometimes coordinating with Soviet forces.

12.1.2 Soviet Support

When the Soviet army rolled into Manchuria in 1945, it recognized Kim Il Sung among other Korean fighters who had been trained in the Soviet Far East. Moscow viewed him as a reliable ally who could help establish a friendly government in northern Korea.

12.1.3 Image Building

After 1945, propaganda highlighted Kim's exploits, glorifying them in newspapers, speeches, and later textbooks. While there was truth to his participation in the resistance, some details were embellished or unverifiable. This "heroic biography" would become the foundation of his cult of personality.

12.2 Consolidating Power Among Rivals

When Kim Il Sung arrived in Pyongyang after liberation, he was not the only influential figure in the northern communist circles. Others had different backgrounds and loyalties: some had worked underground in Korea, some had links to Chinese communist forces, and some were local nationalists with no direct ties to Moscow.

12.2.1 Key Rival Factions

1. **Domestic Communists**: People like Kim Tu-bong or Choe Yong-gon had stayed in Korea during the colonial era, building local networks. They sometimes viewed Soviet-returned communists like Kim Il Sung with suspicion.
2. **Yan'an Faction**: Another group had served with Chinese communists in Yan'an (China). They had strong ties to Mao Zedong's forces and had their own heroes and leadership.
3. **Soviet-Koreans**: Koreans who had grown up in the Soviet Union or fought alongside the Red Army, sometimes more fluent in Russian than Korean. They were loyal to Moscow but not necessarily to Kim Il Sung personally.

12.2.2 Kim Il Sung's Strategy

Kim cultivated support from Soviet authorities, who helped him outmaneuver or sideline rivals. He offered some positions to them but kept the most critical roles—like control of the security apparatus and the propaganda machinery—under his influence. Gradually, as the DPRK formed, Kim placed his allies in top positions.

12.2.3 Suppressing Opposition

Leaders who openly challenged Kim risked being labeled reactionary or "factional." Some were removed from posts or forced into lesser roles. By the late 1940s, Kim had become the undisputed figurehead, though major factional purges would happen more forcefully in later years. At this stage, he needed to keep some semblance of unity, especially with the threat of war looming.

12.3 The Rise of a Personality Cult

Even in these early years, signs of a personality cult around Kim Il Sung appeared. This would later become a hallmark of North Korean politics, but its roots can be traced back to the late 1940s.

12.3.1 Media Portrayals

Newspapers, radio programs, and public rallies praised Kim Il Sung as the "Sun of the Nation," an apt metaphor that suggested he gave light and life to the people. Stories of his guerrilla feats played repeatedly, often with dramatic flair.

12.3.2 Public Rituals

Events like Kim Il Sung's birthday or the anniversaries of key battles were marked with parades and ceremonies. Children were taught to sing songs about his leadership, while adults attended speeches that framed Kim as the guardian of Korean independence.

12.3.3 Early Devotion and Fear

Most ordinary people had little chance to doubt these stories. The new government provided land and jobs, telling them these gains were thanks to Kim's leadership. Publicly questioning him could attract suspicion. Over time, the combination of reverence and fear cemented his authority.

12.4 Relations with Moscow and Beijing

As leader of the DPRK, Kim Il Sung needed to balance relationships with the Soviet Union and the newly established People's Republic of China (PRC). Both were huge neighbors with significant influence.

12.4.1 Soviet Priority

Initially, the USSR was the more dominant partner. It had stationed troops in the north from 1945 to 1948, trained the KPA, and supported Kim's early rule. Kim often visited the Soviet Union for talks, learning about Stalin's economic and political methods.

12.4.2 China's Rise

When Mao Zedong declared the PRC in October 1949, China became another major communist power on Korea's doorstep. Kim Il Sung recognized the potential for Chinese support, especially if conflict with the south escalated. Some members of the DPRK leadership had deep ties with Chinese communists, which Kim had to manage carefully.

12.4.3 Competing Influences

While both the USSR and PRC favored a socialist Korea, they each wanted to shape the DPRK in ways that served their interests. Kim skillfully played them against each other, securing aid from both sides. Even in these early years, he showed a knack for navigating between bigger communist powers.

12.5 Building the Economy and Society

Before outright conflict erupted, Kim Il Sung focused on building a socialist economy in the north, continuing policies begun right after liberation.

12.5.1 Industrial Drive

Factories nationalized under the new regime needed skilled workers, raw materials, and updated machinery. Soviet advisors provided some modern equipment and technical knowledge. Kim encouraged rapid growth, setting production targets that factories struggled to meet.

- **Heavy Industry Focus**: The leadership believed steel, machinery, and chemicals were the backbone of a strong socialist state. Consumer goods received less attention, causing shortages of everyday items.

12.5.2 Agricultural Adjustments

While land reform had been popular, the government was already considering steps toward cooperative farming, in which families would pool land and labor. By 1949–1950, some pilot cooperatives appeared, but the state stopped short of forcing everyone into large collectives—perhaps because it did not want to upset newly contented peasants just yet.

12.5.3 Social Welfare

The DPRK introduced free education and some forms of medical care. Though limited and facing resource constraints, these measures won support among the poor, who had never seen such services under Japanese rule. Schools taught a curriculum that included science, Marxist-Leninist ideology, and praise for Kim Il Sung. Hospitals were small and understaffed, but still a step forward from the colonial era's neglect of Korean health needs.

12.6 Preparing for Reunification: The Road to War

From the start, Kim Il Sung and his government viewed the south as part of the same nation. Official statements called Syngman Rhee's government "illegitimate" and promised that true national unity would come under the DPRK. But how would that unity be achieved?

12.6.1 Internal Discussion of Armed Struggle

Behind closed doors, Kim Il Sung and top officials considered a military option. They believed southern citizens were oppressed by landlords and pro-Japanese collaborators. According to Kim's reasoning, if the KPA crossed the border, southerners might rise up in support of the north.

12.6.2 Stalin's Hesitation

Kim Il Sung needed Soviet approval before launching any major attack. Initially, Joseph Stalin was cautious. He worried that an invasion might trigger a larger conflict with the United States. However, by early 1950, Stalin's stance seemed to soften, possibly because the Soviets had tested their first atomic bomb and were more confident about confronting the West.

12.6.3 China's Role

Kim also consulted Mao Zedong. Mao, fresh from victory in the Chinese Civil War, was open to supporting the DPRK but did not want to provoke the U.S. unnecessarily. Still, the idea of a strong, communist-led peninsula appealed to him, especially if it meant pushing American influence out of East Asia.

12.7 Politicizing the Military

In many socialist countries, the ruling party maintains tight control over the armed forces. Kim Il Sung was no exception. He saw the KPA not just as a defense force but also as a tool for spreading communist ideology.

- **Political Commissars**: Units had commissars to ensure loyalty to the party. They led study sessions on Marxist-Leninist ideas and Kim Il Sung's teachings.
- **Training**: Soldiers were drilled in modern tactics learned from Soviet instructors. They practiced crossing rivers and coordinating tank-infantry assaults—skills that would become crucial if they moved south.

As the KPA grew stronger, Kim's confidence in a swift victory over the south also grew.

12.8 Diplomatic Moves and Propaganda

Even while preparing militarily, Kim Il Sung used diplomacy and propaganda to claim the moral high ground. He often proposed "peaceful" or "democratic" solutions that implicitly favored the DPRK's system.

12.8.1 Joint Elections?

In early 1950, the DPRK suggested holding all-Korean elections to form a single government. But the conditions they set—like allowing free political activity for leftists in the south—were unacceptable to Syngman Rhee, who viewed them as a communist tactic to undermine his regime.

12.8.2 Radio and Leaflets

The north's radio stations broadcast across the border, urging southerners to resist Rhee's government and join the "people's cause." Leaflets were sometimes dropped from balloons or smuggled in, promising that unification under the DPRK would bring land reform and freedom from American control.

12.8.3 International Showcasing

To the broader socialist world, the DPRK portrayed itself as a successful example of post-colonial transformation, a model for other nations shaking off imperialism. This helped rally moral and material support from fellow communist states.

12.9 The Domestic Outlook: Ambition and Risk

Inside the DPRK, enthusiasm for continued reforms clashed with the looming possibility of war. Factories increased output, soldiers drilled, and propaganda urged everyone to prepare for the "final battle" to liberate the south. Yet many families likely felt anxious, recalling the brutality of past conflicts.

12.9.1 Early Economic Strains

Despite upbeat propaganda, the economy was under strain. Some resources had to be diverted to military production. Consumer goods were scarce, and rationing began in some areas. The government often blamed sabotage or the "U.S.-controlled south" for shortages.

12.9.2 Heightened Surveillance

As tensions rose, the state cracked down on any dissent. Neighborhood watch committees reported suspicious talk. People who questioned the government's direction or who had ties to the south might be branded spies. This environment of fear and control helped solidify Kim Il Sung's power but also limited free discussion of policy.

12.9.3 Hope for a Quick Victory

Meanwhile, state media claimed the DPRK's forces, motivated by socialist ideals, would quickly triumph if war started. The image of unstoppable progress fed a widespread belief that southern citizens would welcome the KPA with open arms. Kim Il Sung's leadership was presented as the deciding factor that would bring about reunification.

12.10 The Outbreak of the Korean War (June 1950)

Though this chapter focuses on Kim Il Sung's early leadership rather than the war itself (which we will detail in Chapter 13), we must touch on how these events culminated in open conflict. In June 1950, DPRK forces crossed the 38th Parallel, igniting a war that would devastate the peninsula.

12.10.1 Planning the Attack

Scholars debate the exact timeline of Kim Il Sung's preparations. But it is clear that by spring 1950, he believed the KPA was strong enough to unify Korea swiftly. Stalin gave a cautious green light, and Mao did not object, provided that success seemed likely.

12.10.2 Rapid Advance

On June 25, 1950, the northern army launched a massive offensive. Within days, they captured Seoul, taking the southern government by surprise. Propaganda announced a great liberation was underway. However, the U.S. and U.N. soon intervened, bringing their forces to defend the south.

12.10.3 Kim's Expectations vs. Reality

Kim Il Sung expected an easy victory. He and his advisors underestimated both southern resistance and the scale of U.S. involvement. This miscalculation would turn the conflict into a long, destructive war rather than a quick, triumphant march.

12.11 The Early War and Kim's Leadership Challenges

As fighting intensified, Kim Il Sung faced new leadership tests. While these events will be covered more fully in the next chapter, it is worth noting some immediate pressures:

- **Military Coordination**: Kim had to coordinate with Soviet and Chinese advisors in real time.
- **Civilian Management**: Bombing raids and front-line shifts forced the government to relocate and manage refugees, even as they tried to keep propaganda messages strong.
- **Factional Tensions**: The war environment gave Kim reason to clamp down further on any political rivals, accusing them of disloyalty if they questioned the war's conduct.

Despite initial advances, the conflict soon swung back and forth, showing Kim that the south, backed by the U.S., would not collapse easily.

12.12 Evolving Ideological Themes

During these early war months, Kim Il Sung's speeches and writings emphasized two major themes:

1. **Anti-Imperialism**: He portrayed the U.S. as the main imperialist threat, overshadowing the internal Korean divide. By fighting the south, the DPRK was (in his narrative) fighting American colonial ambitions.

2. **Korean Unity**: He insisted that the "Southern brothers" longed for the DPRK's leadership. Any sign of southern resistance was blamed on reactionary elites or foreign meddling. This messaging tried to maintain morale among DPRK troops and citizens, who might otherwise question why many southerners did not immediately welcome them.

12.13 Kim Il Sung's Personal Traits and Leadership Style

Accounts from people who worked closely with Kim Il Sung in this period describe him as:

- **Confident and Persuasive**: Skilled at winning people over with a friendly demeanor, while keeping a firm grip on power behind the scenes.
- **Quick to Adapt**: Willing to change tactics if he sensed an opportunity—such as pivoting from land reform to war mobilization without hesitation.
- **Prone to Political Calculation**: Maintaining alliances with Soviet and Chinese leaders required delicate maneuvering. Kim displayed an ability to flatter them when needed, but also stood firm on certain points to show he was a strong leader, not merely a puppet.

This blend of charm, cunning, and ideological zeal helped him survive the early, chaotic years of the DPRK's existence.

12.14 Public Perception in the North

Ordinary people in the north likely had varied opinions on Kim Il Sung's rule. Some saw him as a genuine liberator who ended centuries of landlord abuse and Japanese cruelty. Others, especially those who lost property or faced purges, quietly resented the new regime but dared not speak out.

- **Widespread Loyalty**: Landless peasants and many young workers, for instance, felt they owed their improved status to the party. They joined mass rallies with genuine enthusiasm.
- **Lingering Doubt**: Families with religious ties or connections to southern relatives might harbor doubts about the war or about Kim's total control. But open dissent could lead to dire consequences.

As the conflict continued, propaganda hammered home the message that Kim Il Sung was the fatherly protector of the north, guiding them through a difficult struggle.

12.15 Strengthening the Police and Security Apparatus

A crucial aspect of Kim Il Sung's leadership was expanding the security forces. Even before the Korean War, special police units were formed to root out "enemies of the revolution."

- **Political Police (Bowibu)**: Tasked with tracking down spies, traitors, and anyone who spread "counter-revolutionary" ideas.
- **Neighborhood Monitoring**: Residents were encouraged (or pressured) to report suspicious behavior. Fear of being denounced kept many people cautious in their speech and actions.
- **Labor Camps**: Early forms of labor camps appeared for those deemed enemies of the state. While these were relatively small at first, the concept of punishing political offenders through forced labor was introduced early on.

Such measures ensured Kim Il Sung faced little organized opposition, helping cement his control.

12.16 Transition to All-Out War

By mid-1950, the newly minted DPRK was consumed by war efforts. Kim Il Sung had gambled on a quick victory, but the Korean War soon turned into a massive international conflict, with the U.S. and other United Nations forces siding with the south, and later China intervening on the north's side.

12.16.1 Evacuation and Relocation

As U.N. forces advanced north in late 1950, the DPRK government evacuated Pyongyang. Kim Il Sung and his top officials moved around to avoid capture, coordinating from hidden locations. This tested the unity of the new state, as chaos and panic spread among civilians.

12.16.2 Deepened Repression

Concerned about spies or sabotage, the government tightened security measures. Large numbers of suspects were arrested or executed, often without fair trials. Even some within the party who voiced concerns about military strategy were purged.

12.16.3 The Role of Chinese "Volunteers"

When Chinese forces entered the war to help the north, Kim Il Sung had to share some control of military operations with Chinese commanders. He faced a delicate balance: welcoming the help but not wanting to appear overshadowed. The presence of massive Chinese troops also forced Kim to reassure his citizens that Korea was still sovereign, even amid foreign armies.

12.17 Setting the Stage for a Long Regime

Despite the devastations of war, Kim Il Sung's early leadership style and policies laid foundations that would endure after the armistice in 1953:

1. **Centralized Power**: Through purges and control of the security apparatus, Kim built a system where his word was law.
2. **State-Directed Economy**: The combination of land reform, nationalized industry, and an emphasis on heavy industry became long-term pillars of North Korea's development strategy.
3. **Propaganda and Personality Cult**: Every success was credited to Kim's leadership, while failures were blamed on external enemies or traitors.
4. **Reunification Ideology**: Kim and his government maintained that the south remained an occupied territory. This claim would shape the north's foreign policy and internal propaganda for decades.

As the war raged on, Kim's standing among the populace—reinforced by intense propaganda—only grew, even as destruction swept the land. Once a peace agreement was finally signed, Kim Il Sung would use both the war's legacy and the continuing Cold War environment to further consolidate his regime.

CHAPTER 13

THE KOREAN WAR (1950–1953)

Introduction

The Korean War began in June 1950 and lasted until July 1953. It was a major conflict that drew in powerful countries from around the world, even though the main fighting took place on the Korean Peninsula. In the north, Kim Il Sung had hoped for a quick victory to reunify the country under his rule. In the south, President Syngman Rhee saw the invasion as a chance to crush communism if the tide could be turned. Meanwhile, the United States, the Soviet Union, and the newly formed People's Republic of China became involved, turning what many expected to be a short civil conflict into a large-scale war.

In this chapter, we will look at the events of the Korean War in a step-by-step manner. We will see how the war started, the reasons behind it, the key battles and turning points, and how everyday people suffered. We will also explore how the war ended in a ceasefire rather than a peace treaty, leaving the peninsula divided. Although we will focus on the northern perspective, we will also discuss the role of foreign armies and how this conflict changed the path of both North and South Korea for decades to come.

13.1 Prelude to War

By mid-1950, Korea was split into two states: the Democratic People's Republic of Korea (DPRK) in the north and the Republic of Korea (ROK) in the south. Each claimed to be the only legitimate government for the entire peninsula. Tensions had been rising along the 38th Parallel for months, with skirmishes happening frequently.

13.1.1 The DPRK's Confidence

Kim Il Sung believed that the south's Syngman Rhee government was unpopular and would collapse if northern forces attacked. Northern propaganda said that southern citizens would welcome the Korean People's Army (KPA) as liberators. The north also had support from the Soviet Union in terms of weapons and training. Some advisors from China, newly under communist rule, also leaned toward helping if a war broke out.

13.1.2 The South's Position

Despite being attacked in smaller border clashes, the south was not fully prepared for a large-scale invasion. Its army was smaller and less equipped. However, the south had the potential backing of the United States, which was worried about communist expansion in Asia. By 1950, the Cold War between the U.S. and the Soviet Union had grown intense, and neither side wanted to lose ground in a key region like Korea.

13.1.3 The Role of Foreign Powers

Before the war began, Kim Il Sung sought approval from Soviet leader Joseph Stalin and at least an understanding with Chinese leader Mao Zedong. Stalin was cautious but eventually gave a limited green light, especially after the Soviet Union's first successful nuclear test in 1949. Mao was also cautious, but he did not openly oppose Kim's plan, possibly believing that if the war succeeded quickly, it would strengthen the communist bloc in East Asia.

13.2 Outbreak of War: June 25, 1950

On June 25, 1950, North Korean forces crossed the 38th Parallel in a surprise attack. Kim Il Sung announced that the south had initiated hostilities, but most evidence suggests the DPRK launched the main offensive.

13.2.1 Rapid Northern Advance

With superior organization, armor, and artillery, the KPA pushed south quickly. Many South Korean units were overwhelmed. In the first few days, the north captured the capital city of Seoul, which was a significant psychological blow to the south.

13.2.2 International Reaction

The United Nations Security Council, in the absence of the Soviet representative (who was boycotting the council at the time), condemned the DPRK's invasion. The U.N. called for member nations to assist South Korea. The United States, under President Harry Truman, led the response and began sending troops and supplies to help the south. Other countries, including Britain, Australia, Canada, and more, joined what became known as the U.N. Command.

13.2.3 Hopes for a Quick Victory

Kim Il Sung and his generals believed they could defeat the south before major U.S. forces could intervene. Propaganda told northern soldiers that they would be greeted as heroes. However, as American troops landed and helped stabilize South Korean defenses, a short victory became less likely.

13.3 Early Battles and Key Turning Points

The war can be roughly divided into several phases, starting with the northern advance, followed by a southern-U.N. counterattack, then a Chinese intervention, and finally a stalemate near the original dividing line.

13.3.1 The Pusan Perimeter (Summer 1950)

North Korean forces swept through most of the south by August 1950, pushing South Korean and U.N. defenders into a small zone around the port city of Pusan in the southeast corner of the peninsula. This became known as the Pusan Perimeter.

- **DPRK's Overreach**: The KPA extended their supply lines and faced logistical struggles. They also encountered heavier U.S. firepower than anticipated.
- **U.N. Reinforcement**: U.N. Command poured men and weapons into Pusan, building strong defensive lines. KPA offensives eventually stalled in the face of superior equipment and air support used by the U.S. Air Force.

13.3.2 The Inchon Landing (September 1950)

General Douglas MacArthur, leading the U.N. forces, planned a bold amphibious landing at Inchon, near Seoul. On September 15, 1950, U.S. Marines and other troops stormed ashore, quickly recapturing Seoul and cutting off many DPRK units from their supply routes.

- **DPRK Retreat**: With enemies now behind them, much of the KPA in the south had to withdraw quickly. Some units were trapped and destroyed.
- **Crossing the 38th Parallel**: U.N. and South Korean forces then went on the offensive, crossing into the north in October. This reversed the war's momentum entirely.

13.3.3 Pyongyang Falls

The U.N. forces captured Pyongyang in late October 1950. For a brief moment, it looked as though the north might be overrun. Kim Il Sung and the DPRK government evacuated the capital, moving further north toward the Yalu River, which separates Korea from China.

13.4 Chinese Intervention: Late 1950

One of the biggest surprises of the war was the massive entry of Chinese "Volunteers" on the side of North Korea. The Chinese leadership feared a U.S.-led force would not stop at the Yalu River and might threaten Chinese territory.

13.4.1 The Crossing of the Yalu

Hundreds of thousands of Chinese troops poured across the Yalu in late October and early November 1950. Their presence was at first hidden, but soon became clear when U.N. units advanced too far north and encountered fierce counterattacks.

13.4.2 Battle of the Chosin Reservoir

A famous engagement involved U.S. Marines and other U.N. forces near the Chosin Reservoir in the mountainous north. The Chinese surrounded them in harsh winter conditions. Though the U.N. troops broke out, they had to retreat south, losing much equipment and suffering heavy casualties.

13.4.3 Reclaiming the North's Territory

With Chinese help, the KPA regained strength. By early 1951, combined DPRK-Chinese forces recaptured Pyongyang, pushing U.N. forces back down past the 38th Parallel. Seoul changed hands multiple times, causing massive disruption for civilians.

13.5 Stalemate and Brutal Warfare

By mid-1951, the front lines settled roughly around the original dividing line. Neither side could make a decisive push. The Korean War devolved into trench-like warfare with heavy artillery, air raids, and high casualties.

13.5.1 Bombing Campaigns in the North

U.S. air power targeted the north's cities, industries, and infrastructure. Pyongyang, Hamhung, and other major locations were heavily bombed, sometimes flattened entirely. Dams, rail lines, and roads were also destroyed. Northern propaganda labeled these actions as evidence of "American imperialist brutality." Civilians suffered greatly, with many homes and entire towns wiped out.

13.5.2 Chinese and KPA Offensives

The Chinese "human wave" attacks and KPA ground assaults inflicted heavy casualties on U.N. forces. However, they also suffered huge losses due to superior U.N. firepower and air strikes. The war's front lines barely moved, even though tens of thousands of soldiers died on both sides.

13.5.3 Civilian Hardship

For ordinary Koreans in both the north and south, the war was a nightmare. Families fled bombs or ground fighting, leading to massive refugee movements. In the north, many sought shelter in caves, mountains, or any remaining villages less targeted by air raids. Food became scarce as farmland was devastated. Disease spread easily in crowded conditions.

13.6 Armistice Talks and the Final Year

As the death toll climbed, all sides eventually realized a military victory was unlikely. Talks began in 1951 near the town of Panmunjom, close to the front lines. But progress was slow, especially over issues like prisoner exchanges.

13.6.1 Key Sticking Points

- **Prisoners of War (POWs)**: Thousands of Chinese and North Korean POWs did not want to return to their homelands. The U.N. Command insisted on voluntary repatriation, while the north and China demanded all POWs be sent back.
- **Demarcation Line**: Another argument was about the final boundary. Both sides wanted to negotiate from positions of strength.

13.6.2 Kim Il Sung's Role

Kim Il Sung had to rely on Soviet and Chinese support during these negotiations. Although he was the head of the DPRK, real power in armistice talks often rested with Soviet and Chinese representatives. Still, Kim stayed committed to continuing the war until a satisfactory deal was reached or a forced reunification seemed impossible.

13.6.3 Final Agreement

After two years of talks, the armistice was finally signed on July 27, 1953. It established a new demilitarized zone (DMZ) near the 38th Parallel, though the line was adjusted slightly based on battle outcomes. However, no formal peace treaty was signed, meaning the war technically never ended.

13.7 The War's Impact on North Korea

The Korean War left deep scars on the northern landscape and population. While the entire peninsula suffered, the north was heavily bombed, losing much of its infrastructure.

13.7.1 Destruction of Cities and Factories

Pyongyang was reduced to rubble, and many other cities faced a similar fate. Factories and mines that had been nationalized after liberation were destroyed or severely damaged, setting back industrial progress. Millions of civilians were homeless.

13.7.2 Heavy Casualties

Exact numbers are debated, but the combined North Korean and Chinese military casualties were vast. Civilians also died in large numbers. Entire generations were traumatized by bombings and the terror of sudden attacks.

13.7.3 Strengthening Kim Il Sung's Power

Despite the chaos, or perhaps partly because of it, Kim Il Sung ended the war with more control than ever. He portrayed himself as the heroic defender of the fatherland who stood against the "American invaders." The war's hardships allowed him to argue that North Koreans must unite under strong leadership for survival.

13.8 The International Context

The Korean War confirmed the global significance of the Cold War. The U.S. saw Korea as a frontline against communism. The Soviet Union and China saw it as a test of their resolve against Western influence in Asia. Thus, the conflict in Korea stood as a key example of how local struggles could become international crises.

13.8.1 Legacy for the U.N.

The war marked the first time a U.N.-mandated force went into large-scale combat. Supporters said it demonstrated U.N. unity against aggression. Critics argued that the absence of Soviet input (due to the boycott) skewed the U.N. decision.

13.8.2 China's Rise in Status

China's involvement showed that it could project military force beyond its borders. The Chinese army, though suffering tremendous losses, proved able to counter a Western-led coalition. This boosted China's standing in the communist world.

13.8.3 Post-War Alliances

After the war, the division on the peninsula became more entrenched. The DPRK leaned heavily on the Soviet Union and later China for post-war rebuilding, while the ROK became an ally of the U.S. This set the stage for ongoing rivalry, fueled by the broader East-West split.

13.9 War Strategies and Their Lessons

While the Korean War ended in a stalemate, each side drew lessons:

- **DPRK**: Kim Il Sung realized that underestimating foreign backing for the south was a major mistake. The north also understood the power of U.S. air support. Going forward, North Korea would build underground facilities and invest in air defenses.

- **South Korea and the U.S.**: They learned that ignoring the possibility of an invasion could be disastrous. U.S. policymakers also recognized the risk of Chinese intervention in Asian conflicts.
- **China**: It learned it could stand up to Western forces in a limited war, though at great cost. China also saw the value of a buffer state on its border, reinforcing the special relationship with North Korea.

These lessons shaped military planning, alliances, and how each side viewed the other for many years after 1953.

13.10 Humanitarian Crisis and Civilian Suffering

From Pyongyang to Pusan, everyday Koreans endured enormous hardship. The war caused widespread famine, disease, and the breakdown of normal life.

13.10.1 Refugee Problems

Families were split apart as people fled bombed-out cities or areas where fighting moved quickly. Some ended up in refugee camps run by the U.N. in the south, or hidden in remote northern mountain regions.

13.10.2 Orphans and Widows

The war left countless orphans and widows in the north. The DPRK government tried to set up orphanages and women's organizations to handle these crises. Propaganda presented Kim Il Sung as a caring "father figure" to war orphans, though resources were severely limited.

13.10.3 Lost Homes and Rebuilding Challenges

Once the bombing stopped, many people returned to find only ruins where their houses once stood. Rebuilding seemed overwhelming, especially with no immediate help from the outside world. The north had to rely on aid from fellow socialist countries, which would come in the following years.

13.11 Prisoners of War and Forced Conversions

During the war, both sides captured thousands of soldiers. The question of what to do with POWs became a central topic at the armistice talks.

- **Communist POWs**: Some North Korean and Chinese POWs did not want to return home, fearing punishment or disillusioned with their cause.
- **U.N./South Korean POWs**: Some had been forced to join the KPA or were re-captured civilians.
- **Repatriation or Defection**: The principle of "voluntary repatriation" ended up being a compromise, allowing some POWs to stay in the south or go to neutral countries.

This complicated issue reflected the deep emotional impact of the conflict. Individuals caught in the war's politics had to make life-changing decisions about where they wanted to live.

13.12 Changing Views of Kim Il Sung's Leadership

Before the war, some North Koreans might have questioned Kim's ambitions or disliked certain reforms. However, during the war, the government's tight control of information and the rallying cry to defend the homeland increased his support base.

13.12.1 Portrayal as a Wartime Leader

North Korean newspapers praised Kim Il Sung's "brilliant tactics," even when the KPA faced defeats. Any problems were blamed on outside factors or on traitors within the ranks. As time went on, the myth of Kim's genius grew.

13.12.2 Factional Tensions and Purges

Under wartime conditions, Kim had a tool to purge or silence rival communist factions. Anyone who doubted him could be accused of sabotage or failing to support the war effort. This pattern of using crises to consolidate power would continue after the war, shaping North Korea's political culture for decades.

13.13 The Path to an Armistice

Negotiations that began in 1951 dragged on, partly because each side tried to gain an advantage on the battlefield to strengthen its position at the table. The change of leadership in key countries also mattered: Joseph Stalin died in March 1953, leading the Soviet Union to push for a quicker end to the conflict.

13.13.1 Final Push for a Ceasefire

After months of intense fighting, both sides agreed that more conflict could only lead to more destruction without real gain. The armistice was signed on July 27, 1953, at Panmunjom.

13.13.2 The Demilitarized Zone (DMZ)

A 4-kilometer-wide DMZ was established around the line of contact. To this day, it remains one of the most heavily fortified borders in the world. The armistice also created the Military Armistice Commission to oversee compliance, but the political issues that caused the war were not resolved.

13.13.3 No Formal Peace Treaty

Crucially, the DPRK, ROK, and other parties never signed a permanent peace treaty. Technically, the war remains ongoing, with only an armistice halting the fighting. This condition has shaped North Korea's internal and external policies ever since.

13.14 Aftermath: Victory or Draw?

In the official narrative of the DPRK, the war's outcome was seen as a victory for Korean independence, preventing the U.S. from conquering the north. However, the final borders barely moved from where they were in 1950, and the country lay in ruins.

13.14.1 Propaganda Celebrations

Kim Il Sung's government claimed that the KPA, supported by Chinese volunteers, had stood up to the "aggressors" and saved Korean sovereignty. Annual celebrations commemorated the war's end, praising heroic feats and the leadership that "defended the homeland."

13.14.2 Deeper Division

On the other hand, the war solidified the division between north and south. Families remained separated, with little hope for reconciliation. Both governments built societies that were hostile to each other, each convinced of its own legitimacy.

13.14.3 Seeds of Future Conflict

The bitterness and devastation from the war also fed future tensions. Both Koreas spent decades militarizing further, living under the constant threat of another invasion. The lasting hostility became a defining feature of North Korea's outlook on the world.

13.15 The War's Effects on the North Korean Mindset

The war cemented certain beliefs within the DPRK's leadership and society:

1. **Suspicion of Foreign Powers**: North Korean officials concluded that Western nations, especially the U.S., would do anything to destroy their country. This justified a permanent state of military readiness.
2. **Reliance on Self**: The war's destruction and limited outside help (beyond Soviet or Chinese military aid) reinforced the idea that North Koreans must rely on themselves—a theme that later grew into the Juche ideology.
3. **Glorification of Kim Il Sung**: Surviving the war and retaining control of the north boosted Kim's heroic status, giving him leeway to shape society in the years that followed.

Over time, these beliefs evolved into guiding principles for the entire country.

13.16 The Human Cost and Legacy

It is important to remember that behind every policy decision and propaganda campaign were real human lives. The war's brutality and the large-scale bombings caused immense tragedy.

- **Casualties**: Estimates vary, but the total number of Korean military and civilian casualties on both sides likely exceeded two million.
- **Orphans and Rebuilding**: Thousands of orphans in the north grew up in state-run facilities, hearing only official stories of the war. Their personal losses shaped how they viewed the outside world.
- **Monuments and Memorials**: After the war, the DPRK erected statues and memorial sites, such as in Pyongyang, to honor fallen soldiers and celebrate wartime heroes. These monuments also served to legitimize the ruling party and Kim Il Sung's leadership.

13.17 Impact on Kim Il Sung's Policies Going Forward

Following the armistice, Kim Il Sung directed North Korea's recovery in a way that reflected lessons from the war:

- **Heavy Emphasis on Defense**: Building a strong military remained a top priority, overshadowing consumer goods production.
- **Centralized Leadership**: Kim used the war's outcome to purge more rivals and justify strict top-down control.
- **Shaping National Identity**: The government portrayed the entire population as soldiers in a continued struggle, even in peacetime, a mindset that would define the DPRK for decades.

This approach carried into the post-war reconstruction era, which we will examine in the next chapter.

CHAPTER 14

REBUILDING AFTER THE WAR

Introduction

When the Korean War armistice came into effect on July 27, 1953, North Korea lay in ruins. Its cities were shattered from intense bombing, fields were scorched, and infrastructure like roads and bridges lay in pieces. However, under the leadership of Kim Il Sung, the country embarked on a massive reconstruction project. This was not just a physical rebuilding but also a chance to remake society according to socialist principles.

In this chapter, we will explore how North Korea tackled post-war recovery and the efforts to build a new economy and social system. We will see how alliances with the Soviet Union and other socialist countries shaped development, and we will examine how Kim Il Sung used this period to strengthen his hold on power. Finally, we will look at how everyday people experienced the challenges and changes that came with building a new society from the rubble.

14.1 The War's Devastation: A Starting Point

The armistice left the north and south roughly divided along the same line as before the war, but the damage in the north was immense.

14.1.1 Destroyed Cities

Pyongyang, once the political and cultural center of the north, was heavily bombed. The city lost most of its buildings. Other towns, like Wonsan, Hamhung, and Chongjin, also suffered massive destruction.

14.1.2 Infrastructure Collapse

Bridges, railways, and factories were prime targets during the war, leaving the north with few operational tracks or manufacturing plants. Many mines were flooded or caved in.

14.1.3 Homeless and Displaced People

Countless families, having fled the fighting, returned to find no homes. Large parts of the population needed emergency shelter, food supplies, and medical care. The government had to address immediate humanitarian needs while planning for long-term rebuilding.

14.2 The Early Reconstruction Policy: Quick Steps to Recovery

As soon as the war ended, Kim Il Sung's government announced a grand drive to rebuild the north. This campaign had both practical and symbolic importance: it aimed to restore everyday life while proving that socialism could overcome massive obstacles.

14.2.1 Mass Mobilization

North Korean propaganda called on every citizen to join "battlefields of construction." Workers, peasants, and students were organized into brigades that cleared debris, rebuilt roads, and repaired rail lines. Volunteer labor became a crucial factor in early recovery.

- **Youth Brigades**: Young people were especially targeted by slogans encouraging them to devote their energy to "build the fatherland." In exchange, they received praise, recognition, and sometimes small incentives.

14.2.2 Soviet and Eastern Bloc Aid

While the U.S. and Western powers helped rebuild South Korea, the DPRK turned to the Soviet Union and other socialist countries for assistance. They provided machinery, technical expertise, and financial loans to jumpstart reconstruction projects.

- **Technical Advisors**: Soviet engineers arrived to help design new factories and rebuild old ones. Eastern European countries also sent doctors, teachers, and construction experts.

14.2.3 Rehabilitating Industry

The first priority was to reopen essential industries, like coal mines and power stations, to ensure a stable supply of energy. The government aimed to surpass pre-war production levels quickly to show that socialism was more efficient than capitalism.

14.3 The Five-Year Plans: Structured Economic Goals

By the mid-1950s, North Korea introduced **Five-Year Plans**, a common feature in socialist countries. These plans set targets for industry, agriculture, and social programs.

14.3.1 The First Five-Year Plan (1957–1961)

This plan aimed to restore and expand heavy industry, such as steelmaking, machinery, and chemicals.

- **State Control of Production**: The government owned all major factories and mines. Managers followed central directives on what and how much to produce.
- **High Targets**: Planners set ambitious goals, hoping to double or triple pre-war production in some sectors. Meeting these targets became a matter of national pride.

14.3.2 Emphasis on Heavy Industry

Why focus on heavy industry? Kim Il Sung believed a strong industrial base was key to defending the country and proving socialism's superiority. Consumer goods like clothing or household items were considered secondary, leading to shortages in daily necessities.

14.3.3 Stakhanovite Movement

Following the Soviet example, North Korea introduced "model worker" campaigns. Laborers who exceeded quotas were praised publicly, given awards, and used as symbols of socialist dedication. While this boosted morale for some, it also added pressure on workers to meet unrealistic goals.

14.4 Agricultural Changes: From Private Plots to Cooperatives

During the immediate post-war years, farmers in the north were still mostly working their own land given to them after the earlier land reform. However, the government gradually pushed for **collective farming** to increase efficiency and control.

14.4.1 Introducing Cooperative Farms

Starting around 1954–1955, small groups of farmers formed cooperatives. They pooled their land, tools, and labor, and shared the harvest. Initially, cooperatives were voluntary, but government pressure was strong.

- **Higher-Level Cooperatives**: As time passed, cooperatives expanded into larger units, sometimes encompassing an entire village. The state provided tractors, seeds, and fertilizers, but also demanded strict adherence to production targets.

14.4.2 Government Incentives and Pressure

Farmers who joined cooperatives received certain benefits: easier access to equipment, seeds, and state loans. However, refusing to join could mean being labeled "backward" or "anti-socialist." This dual approach of incentive and intimidation sped up collectivization.

14.4.3 Results for Rural Life

Collective farming changed village structures. Homes remained private, but land was farmed collectively. Some farmers liked the shared labor and guaranteed distribution of harvest. Others missed autonomy and worried about fixed state quotas, which could be high. Over time, the entire countryside adapted to this new system.

14.5 Reconstructing Cities: Modern Layouts and Socialist Style

With many northern cities devastated, urban planning became a priority. The government saw this as a chance to create modern, orderly cities that embodied socialist ideals.

14.5.1 Pyongyang's Transformation

The capital was rebuilt with wide boulevards, large public squares, and monument-style buildings. Apartments were constructed in a grid-like fashion, aiming to provide housing for workers and families close to factories and offices.

- **Monuments**: Statues of war heroes, particularly dedicated to Kim Il Sung, were placed in prominent areas. This combined civic pride with political loyalty.

14.5.2 Public Amenities and Culture

The state tried to include theaters, schools, and sports facilities to encourage a communal spirit. Citizens were organized in local committees to keep streets clean and participate in cultural events.

- **Mass Rallies**: Large squares, such as Kim Il Sung Square, were designed to hold mass rallies where thousands of people could gather for celebrations, parades, or political announcements.

14.5.3 Housing Shortages

Despite these grand plans, many families faced overcrowding. Construction materials were scarce, and new apartments were small. However, compared to the total chaos right after the war, many people saw even a cramped apartment as an improvement.

14.6 Societal Reforms and Education Drive

The DPRK leadership understood that rebuilding a country required not just physical infrastructure but also shaping people's minds and skills.

14.6.1 Expanding Education

Even before the war, literacy campaigns were important. After 1953, the government re-launched efforts to provide free education at all levels.

- **Compulsory Schooling**: Children were required to attend primary and secondary school. This system also included political lessons about the party and Kim Il Sung.
- **Technical Colleges**: To support industrial growth, vocational schools and technical colleges sprang up. They trained machinists, engineers, and other specialists needed in factories.

14.6.2 Health and Welfare

Hospitals, heavily damaged by bombings, were rebuilt with assistance from socialist allies. Public health campaigns targeted common diseases and malnutrition. Though resources were limited, the government emphasized that healthcare was a right, not a luxury.

14.6.3 Women's Roles

Officially, women were encouraged to join the workforce, especially in factories or on cooperative farms. Laws stated that men and women should have equal pay and opportunities. However, many women still faced traditional expectations at home. State propaganda highlighted model women who balanced farm or factory work with household duties.

14.7 Kim Il Sung's Consolidation of Power

While post-war reconstruction brought positive changes for many, it also gave Kim Il Sung the chance to tighten his grip on the political system.

14.7.1 Purging Rival Factions

The war had weakened some of Kim's political rivals. In the mid-to-late 1950s, he targeted remaining factions within the Workers' Party of Korea. Some members who had sided with Soviet or Chinese interests were accused of "factionalism" and removed.

- **August Faction Incident (1956)**: A group of leaders who opposed Kim's growing personality cult attempted to challenge him. Kim struck back swiftly, removing them from power. This event marked a major turning point, leaving Kim unchallenged in the party.

14.7.2 Personality Cult Grows

As reconstruction successes were reported, state media credited Kim Il Sung personally for every gain. Songs, literature, and school lessons praised his wisdom. Over time, this cult of personality became central to North Korean politics, with Kim's image everywhere.

14.7.3 Shifting Away from Soviet Influence

Although the DPRK still needed Soviet aid, Kim wanted to show he was not just a puppet. He began promoting the idea of **Juche**—self-reliance—in official speeches, suggesting that North Korea would forge its own socialist path unique to its conditions.

14.8 Dependence on Foreign Support

Despite the talk of self-reliance, the DPRK relied significantly on aid and loans from the Soviet Union, China, and Eastern Europe. This help was essential to rebuild factories and train experts. However, the government rarely highlighted this dependence in public statements, focusing instead on the heroic efforts of North Koreans.

14.8.1 Soviet Loans and Technology

The Soviets provided equipment for heavy industry, such as turbines for power plants and machinery for steel mills. Technicians visited the north to assist with complex installations.

14.8.2 Chinese Labor Assistance

China also sent construction brigades at times, helping rebuild roads and rail lines near the border. In return, the DPRK provided China with some coal and other resources once its mines were operational again.

14.8.3 Balancing Two Giants

As Sino-Soviet relations later became tense, Kim Il Sung carefully balanced ties with both powers, extracting maximum aid without appearing to favor one side too strongly. This balancing act was a key part of North Korean diplomacy.

14.9 Everyday Life in the Reconstruction Era

How did ordinary North Koreans experience the rebuilding years?

14.9.1 Work and Rationing

Jobs were plentiful because of the need to rebuild. However, wages were controlled by the state. Many goods were distributed through a rationing system. While some essential items were available, variety was limited. For instance, clothing often came in standardized designs, and food supplies were carefully measured.

14.9.2 New Social Groups

Young people who grew up during or right after the war were molded by a strong sense of loyalty to the nation and to Kim Il Sung. Many were enthusiastic about building a new society, joining youth leagues or volunteer projects.

- **Cultural Activities**: Factories and farms often had their own performance troupes or reading clubs. After a day's labor, people would gather to practice patriotic songs or plays, reinforcing community spirit.

14.9.3 Family Reunions?

The war had split many families, with members stuck in the south or missing in the chaos. The new government strongly discouraged any talk of reunifying families except under the north's terms. Communication with relatives in the south became almost impossible, leaving many to grieve lost family connections.

14.10 Shaping the "New Socialist Person"

Along with physical rebuilding, the DPRK government tried to shape citizens into ideal socialist workers, loyal to the party and its leader.

14.10.1 Propaganda Campaigns

Newspapers and radio broadcasts praised model laborers who sacrificed personal comfort for the collective good. Students learned about these role models in school, forming an idea that the highest honor was to serve the state.

14.10.2 Cultural Control

Writers and artists were guided to produce works that promoted socialist realism—stories or paintings of heroic peasants and workers. Folk traditions were allowed if they showed national pride, but anything considered "feudal" or "superstitious" was discouraged.

14.10.3 Surveillance

In local committees, neighbors monitored each other for signs of discontent. The government believed that if someone criticized official policies or showed "wrong thinking," it threatened social unity. Fear of being reported kept many from expressing private doubts.

14.11 Early Signs of Economic Growth

Despite challenges, North Korea saw noticeable progress in its reconstruction efforts by the late 1950s.

- **Industrial Output**: Steel, coal, and electricity production rebounded, surpassing pre-war levels.
- **Agriculture**: Crop yields improved with the adoption of cooperative farming and increased use of machinery and fertilizer.
- **Infrastructure**: Roads, bridges, and rail lines were restored. Pyongyang took shape as a modern, if austere, socialist capital.

This visible improvement made many North Koreans proud, feeding the narrative that their system was superior to the south's.

14.12 Comparing North and South's Reconstruction

South Korea also rebuilt during the same period, but with different strategies and heavy U.S. aid. While it is beyond this book's scope to detail southern development, many in the north believed their progress was more genuinely "national," free from foreign "imperialism." In truth, both Koreas depended on external assistance.

14.13 Managing Expectations and Propaganda

As life stabilized, the government needed to maintain a sense of momentum and keep enthusiasm high. Kim Il Sung frequently toured factories and farms, giving "on-the-spot guidance" to local officials. Photos and articles portrayed him as a caring leader who listened to workers and offered solutions.

- **Challenges**: Not all targets were met. Some factories failed to reach the ambitious quotas set by the Five-Year Plan. Damaged farmland took time to recover fully.

- **Explanations**: Failures were usually blamed on sabotage or the "lingering effects" of war. This narrative helped the leadership avoid admitting any flaws in their system.

14.14 Further Consolidation of One-Party Rule

By the late 1950s, the Worker's Party of Korea was the undisputed authority in the north. Other minor parties existed in name only, serving as tokens of "democratic diversity" while following the WPK's line.

- **National Assembly**: Elections were held for the Supreme People's Assembly, but candidates were typically chosen by the party or mass organizations. Voters had little choice but to support the official list.
- **Social Organizations**: Women's unions, youth leagues, and labor groups all came under party control. Even if they had local leaders, these leaders answered to higher party officials.

This process was mirrored in many socialist nations, but in North Korea, Kim Il Sung's personal influence was becoming uniquely powerful.

14.15 Sino-Soviet Split and North Korea's Position

In the late 1950s, tensions emerged between the Soviet Union (under Nikita Khrushchev) and Mao's China. Each claimed to be the true leader of the communist world. This rivalry put North Korea in a tricky spot.

14.15.1 Kim Il Sung's Diplomacy

Kim tried to stay neutral, avoiding a clear choice between Moscow and Beijing. He praised both countries publicly, accepted aid from both, and criticized neither side openly—at least not yet.

14.15.2 Benefit to the DPRK

Because both superpowers wanted North Korea as an ally, they continued to offer economic and military support. This allowed Kim to extract resources without committing fully to either side's position in the Sino-Soviet argument.

14.15.3 Seeds of Juche

This environment encouraged Kim Il Sung to develop Juche further. He could claim that North Korea was not just following orders from bigger socialist states but forging its own path. This helped him strengthen internal legitimacy and avoid becoming a mere pawn in the larger communist world.

14.16 Everyday Culture and Life Improvement

Although shortages remained, life for many North Koreans slowly improved compared to the war years. People now had more stable housing, children went to school without interruption, and the daily threat of air raids was gone.

14.16.1 Public Festivals

To keep morale high, the government organized regular festivals—like the Day of the Sun (Kim Il Sung's birthday) or other national holidays—featuring parades and performances. These events gave people a sense of shared achievement.

14.16.2 Sports and Activities

In the spirit of mass participation, sports clubs were encouraged at workplaces and schools. Some sports events turned into friendly competitions with neighboring factories or cooperatives, building local pride.

14.16.3 Health Campaigns

Local clinics and mobile medical teams promoted vaccination and basic hygiene. Although limited by resources, these efforts reduced certain diseases, like cholera or smallpox, benefiting rural communities especially.

14.17 Challenges and Complaints

Not everyone was satisfied. Some people complained in private about strict discipline, limited consumer goods, and constant political meetings.

- **Travel Restrictions**: Citizens needed permits to move between cities, limiting personal freedom.
- **Thin Margins for Survival**: Farmers often had to meet high state quotas. If harvests fell short, they had little leftover for themselves.
- **Purges**: Fear of purges or accusations of disloyalty also created a tense atmosphere, discouraging open criticism.

Nevertheless, the official media rarely mentioned such issues, focusing on success stories and examples of "model" citizens.

14.18 Long-Term Significance of Reconstruction

By the early 1960s, the basic foundations of North Korea's socialist system were largely set:

1. **Central Planning**: The state directed industry and agriculture, with five-year plans guiding production.
2. **Collectivized Farming**: Most farmland was under cooperative management, standardizing rural life.
3. **One-Party Rule**: The WPK, under Kim Il Sung, had no serious rivals.
4. **Personality Cult**: Kim was celebrated as the architect of victory over the Japanese, defender in the Korean War, and builder of a new society.

This period laid the groundwork for the next decades of North Korean history, in which the country would further develop its unique blend of socialism, nationalism, and strong leadership. Though everyday life was far from easy, many saw themselves as pioneers of a new era.

14.20 Conclusion

The years after the Korean War were pivotal for North Korea. Although the country was devastated, Kim Il Sung's government turned the crisis into an opportunity to reshape the economy, society, and political structures along strict socialist lines. With the help of Soviet, Chinese, and Eastern European aid—and the tireless efforts of its own citizens—the north rebuilt its cities, reactivated its factories, and launched collective farming. People's lives remained controlled by the party at every turn, with constant propaganda, rationing, and limited freedoms. Yet, in the eyes of many, these hardships were part of creating a proud, independent state that had survived one of the most brutal conflicts of the century.

In our next chapters, we will explore how North Korea continued to evolve under Kim Il Sung's rule, especially with the emergence of Juche as a defining ideology and the impact of the Cold War on the peninsula. The post-war rebuilding stage set the tone for further economic experiments, political purges, and cultural developments that made North Korea unique in the socialist world.

CHAPTER 15

JUCHE IDEOLOGY AND ITS IMPACT

Introduction

By the late 1950s and early 1960s, North Korea had made remarkable progress in rebuilding from the ruins of war. Factories were working again, cities were taking shape, and agriculture had been reorganized into cooperatives. During this period, Kim Il Sung and his government started emphasizing a new guiding principle called **Juche**, which can be translated as "self-reliance" or "main subject." Although the word "Juche" appeared in some official speeches earlier, it was in the 1960s and 1970s that it fully emerged as the central doctrine of the Workers' Party of Korea.

In this chapter, we will look at how Juche became the core ideology of North Korea. We will discuss what Juche means in everyday language, how it shaped politics, the economy, and culture, and why it was so attractive to many people in the north. We will also explore how it gave Kim Il Sung a tighter grip on power, turning him into a figure of near-absolute authority. Finally, we will see the effects of Juche on foreign policy, as North Korea tried to distance itself from both Soviet and Chinese models to create a truly "independent" path.

15.1 The Roots of Juche

North Korean propaganda typically credits Kim Il Sung as the sole creator of Juche. However, like many political ideologies, Juche did not appear overnight. It developed gradually, influenced by global socialism, Korean nationalism, and the intense desire to avoid becoming a puppet of bigger powers.

15.1.1 Anti-Colonial Sentiment

Korea's history of foreign invasions—first by the Japanese and then the heavy involvement of outside forces in the Korean War—led many in the north to distrust foreign interference. People wanted to stand on their own feet, free from any outside control. This sentiment formed a key base for Juche.

15.1.2 Early Speeches by Kim Il Sung

In the 1950s, Kim Il Sung gave speeches urging North Koreans to trust their own strength instead of relying too much on allies like the Soviet Union or China. He mentioned "autonomous politics," "self-reliant economy," and "independent defense." These points would evolve into the more formal Juche ideology.

15.1.3 Inspiration from Global Socialism

At the same time, Juche borrowed ideas from Marxism-Leninism, such as the importance of a vanguard party and state planning. What made it unique was its extreme focus on Korean "self-reliance" over any foreign doctrine. This emphasis let North Korea claim it was following a "Korean-style socialism," not merely copying the Soviets or the Chinese.

15.2 Core Principles of Juche

Over time, official statements crystallized Juche into three main areas: political independence, economic self-sufficiency, and defense autonomy. These areas blended together to form the guiding framework for all aspects of North Korean policy.

15.2.1 Political Independence (Jaju)

Political independence meant the DPRK should decide its own path without bowing to other nations. In practice, this involved discouraging open criticism of the regime, as all decisions were said to be correct if they came from Kim Il Sung and the party. Externally, it meant not letting the Soviet Union or China dictate policy.

15.2.2 Economic Self-Sufficiency (Jarip)

Economic self-sufficiency aimed to build an economy that did not depend on foreign goods, technology, or capital. Officials encouraged local factories to produce everything from machinery to basic consumer goods. North Korea tried to reduce imports and refused to rely on foreign loans. While this boosted national pride, it also sometimes led to shortages of advanced technology and materials.

15.2.3 Defense Autonomy (Jawi)

Defense autonomy called for a strong military capable of deterring any invasion or pressure. This principle was rooted in memories of the Korean War, during which the DPRK had been forced to rely heavily on Chinese "volunteers" and Soviet aid. Kim Il Sung wanted to ensure North Korea could protect itself independently in the future.

15.3 Kim Il Sung's Rise in Status Through Juche

Juche became more than just a political slogan; it turned into a tool that greatly elevated Kim Il Sung's power. By claiming that he alone had discovered and developed this ideology, Kim secured his position as the "Great Leader," the source of all wisdom in the country.

15.3.1 The Leader as the Brain of the Nation

In North Korean propaganda, the party and the people formed the body, while Kim Il Sung was like the brain that guided all actions. Juche teachings said that only through absolute loyalty to him could the people achieve true independence. Over time, this logic justified harsh crackdowns on any dissent.

15.3.2 Personality Cult Expands

Books, newspapers, and school textbooks repeated the story that Kim Il Sung had led the anti-Japanese struggle, saved the country during the Korean War, and given the gift of Juche to the people. Large portraits of Kim Il Sung hung in homes and offices, and mandatory sessions taught that only by following his teachings could North Korea stay strong.

15.3.3 Discrediting Rivals

Inside the Workers' Party, anyone who disagreed or questioned Kim's ideas was branded "anti-Juche" or "pro-foreign." By linking patriotism so closely to loyalty to Kim Il Sung, Juche ideology helped remove all significant opposition. Through multiple purges in the 1950s and 1960s, Kim ensured no serious challenges remained.

15.4 Shaping Domestic Policies

Juche impacted almost every aspect of North Korean life, including economic planning, cultural development, and social programs. It offered a unique lens through which the government set policies.

15.4.1 Economic Self-Reliance in Practice

Factories were encouraged to develop local substitutes for imported materials. For instance, if certain chemicals used in manufacturing came from abroad, scientists were told to find ways to make them domestically. If some machinery needed foreign parts, workshops were tasked with inventing local replacements.

- **Achievements**: This approach spurred creativity and occasional breakthroughs, such as improved local designs for farm equipment. It also built a sense of pride that "we can do it ourselves."
- **Limitations**: North Korea sometimes lagged behind in technology. Without open trade or broad alliances, it was hard to keep up with global advancements.

15.4.2 Cultural Self-Reliance

Artists, writers, and filmmakers were told to create works reflecting North Korean spirit. Western or Soviet cultural forms were acceptable only if they could be adapted to the Juche style. Traditional Korean tales were retold to emphasize moral lessons about loyalty to the leader.

- **Music and Dance**: Folk melodies and dances were reshaped to highlight themes of national pride or success in the fields and factories.

- **Films and Theater**: Popular dramas often showed heroic workers or soldiers who overcame challenges through faith in Juche principles.

15.4.3 Education and Indoctrination

Schools introduced Juche from an early age. Children memorized stories about Kim Il Sung's wisdom. Universities stressed that scientific research must serve the country's self-reliance. While technical skills were important, the ultimate goal was to mold citizens who believed firmly in Juche.

15.5 Foreign Relations Under the Banner of Juche

Internationally, Juche guided how North Korea interacted with both allies and adversaries. The DPRK claimed to be neutral in the Sino-Soviet split, refusing to side openly with either camp. It also insisted on forging ties with non-aligned nations in Asia, Africa, and Latin America.

15.5.1 Balancing Between Moscow and Beijing

With the Soviets and Chinese each hoping to influence North Korea, Juche gave Kim Il Sung a rhetorical tool to say, "We appreciate your help, but we follow our own path." He would accept aid from both but refused to let either overshadow his leadership.

- **Economic Aid**: Both the Soviet Union and China continued sending equipment or loans, not wanting to lose North Korea to the other's sphere.

- **Political Maneuvers**: Kim Il Sung hosted delegations from both countries, showing equal respect in public while maintaining that North Korea's policies were shaped by Juche, not foreign advice.

15.5.2 Relations with Non-Aligned Countries

Countries that had thrown off colonial rulers—like in Africa and parts of Asia—often admired North Korea's stance of strong nationalism. The DPRK offered them scholarships, built cultural exchange programs, and portrayed itself as a model of a small nation standing up to big powers.

15.5.3 Ongoing Hostility with the U.S. and South Korea

From the Juche perspective, the United States was the main imperialist threat, and the South Korean government was viewed as its puppet. Talks of reunification placed Juche at the center—only by following self-reliance, the DPRK claimed, could the Korean people truly be free. Diplomatic relations with the U.S. or the south were minimal or nonexistent, except for occasional negotiations over specific issues.

15.6 Ideological Education and Propaganda

As Juche became the official state ideology, North Korea built an extensive propaganda system to spread its message. Almost every aspect of daily life reinforced Juche lessons.

15.6.1 Publications and Media

Radio broadcasts, television programs, and newspapers repeated speeches and slogans about self-reliance. Weekly political study sessions in workplaces and neighborhoods made sure everyone understood the "correct" line. Repetitive messaging hammered home the belief that Juche was a scientific truth, not just a political stance.

15.6.2 Monuments and Landmarks

In Pyongyang and other cities, large monuments celebrated Juche. For example, the **Juche Tower**, erected in 1982, became a major symbol. It stood tall near the Taedong River, representing the "eternal flame" of North Korean independence. Such structures physically embodied Juche in the urban landscape.

15.6.3 Role of "Ideological Struggle"

Officials insisted that internal and external "class enemies" might still exist, trying to undermine Juche. Citizens were encouraged to be vigilant, reporting suspicious behavior or foreign ideas. This environment fostered fear of being labeled disloyal, leading to strong social conformity.

15.7 Impact on the Economy and Society

Although Juche boosted national pride, it also created obstacles. Insisting on total self-reliance in a modern industrial age often led to inefficiencies and isolation.

15.7.1 Industrial Achievements

In some sectors—like steel production, chemicals, and military hardware—North Korea did manage to build respectable facilities. By the late 1960s, it was outproducing South Korea in heavy industry, at least on paper. This success fed the narrative that Juche was working.

15.7.2 Agricultural Struggles

Farming under a fully self-reliant model had limits. The north's mountainous terrain made large-scale agriculture challenging. Without extensive trade to import fertilizers or modern equipment, yields sometimes lagged. The government tried to develop local fertilizer plants but often faced technical and resource shortages.

15.7.3 Daily Life Sacrifices

Focusing heavily on heavy industry meant fewer consumer goods and limited variety in people's diets, clothing, and household items. State rationing was common. While many citizens remained loyal, privately some wished for better living standards.

15.8 Conflict with Soviet and Chinese Models

By the late 1960s, Kim Il Sung openly distanced North Korea from the orthodox doctrines of both the Soviet Union and Maoist China. He argued that each country's revolution must follow its own path, and for Korea, that path was Juche.

15.8.1 Critique of "Revisionism"

North Korean publications accused the Soviet Union of revisionism, meaning they had abandoned "true" revolutionary principles by pushing peaceful coexistence with the West. This allowed Kim to say North Korea was more revolutionary than Moscow, further fueling national pride.

15.8.2 Avoiding Maoist Extremes

Mao Zedong's Cultural Revolution (launched in 1966) worried Kim Il Sung, as it led to chaos and attacks on established party officials in China. Kim made sure no similar movement arose in North Korea, portraying Juche as a stable and orderly approach, in contrast to the upheaval in China.

15.8.3 Tensions and Reconciliations

Though relationships with both the Soviets and the Chinese had strains, Kim never completely severed ties. He still needed their economic and military support, and they needed North Korea as an ally against the U.S. presence in East Asia. Juche offered a middle ground to claim independence while maintaining alliances on his terms.

15.9 Cultural Expressions of Juche

The arts in North Korea became a way to celebrate and spread Juche ideals. Music, dance, theater, and literature all featured heroic stories of self-reliance and love for the homeland.

15.9.1 Opera and Revolutionary Plays

Operas like **"Sea of Blood"** and **"The Flower Girl"** were performed across the country, depicting poor but virtuous peasants overcoming hardships through unity and faith in the party's leadership. These works were said to be based on Kim Il Sung's teachings, elevating them to near-sacred status.

15.9.2 Fine Arts and Murals

Bright, colorful posters showing farmers, soldiers, or workers always had slogans about Juche. Public murals often featured Kim Il Sung guiding citizens. Paintings rarely showed any sign of doubt or hardship, instead focusing on triumph and positivity.

15.9.3 Large-Scale Mass Games

One striking cultural phenomenon was the **Arirang Mass Games**, giant displays with thousands of performers in synchronized gymnastics or card-flipping shows, forming huge images that glorified the nation and its leader. These events demonstrated collective discipline, symbolizing that under Juche, everyone moved as one.

15.10 Education as a Tool for Ideological Training

From elementary school through university, lessons on Juche were integrated into every subject. Math problems might refer to factory production targets. Language exercises included quotes from Kim Il Sung. University-level studies demanded reading official texts on Juche philosophy.

- **Scholarships and Rewards**: Students who excelled in ideological knowledge, as well as academics, were praised as future leaders.
- **Harsh Punishments**: Those who criticized or asked difficult questions about Juche risked being punished or denied opportunities. This climate suppressed independent thought, ensuring loyalty from an early age.

15.11 Military Emphasis and Songun Tendencies

Though the term "Songun" (military-first) policy became more formal under Kim Jong Il much later, its roots were visible during Kim Il Sung's Juche years. The state continued to invest heavily in defense industries.

15.11.1 Self-Reliance in Armaments

Factories sought to produce tanks, artillery, and even naval vessels. North Korea also aimed to develop ballistic missiles and possibly nuclear technology, believing that real independence required strong military deterrence.

15.11.2 Militia and Citizen-Soldiers

Civilians were encouraged to train in basic military drills. Schoolchildren had paramilitary sessions. By blurring the lines between civilian and soldier, North Korea formed a society on constant alert, ready to mobilize if threatened.

15.12 Criticisms and Contradictions

While Juche succeeded in uniting the population under one ideology, critics argue that it also stifled innovation and created contradictions.

15.12.1 Hidden Dependence on Aid

Despite claims of self-reliance, North Korea still relied on considerable help from socialist allies. Grain and oil imports, along with technical expertise, were often essential. Officials rarely admitted this publicly.

15.12.2 Resource Misallocation

Pushing for self-sufficiency in all areas sometimes meant inefficient use of limited resources. For instance, trying to produce advanced machinery without the right materials or skills could result in substandard goods that slowed industrial growth.

15.12.3 Isolation from Global Knowledge

Rejecting foreign influence kept certain harmful ideas out, but it also cut North Korea off from beneficial scientific or cultural exchanges. Over time, the gap between North Korea's technology and that of more open countries widened.

15.13 Evolution of Juche Over Time

Juche was not static. It evolved as North Korea's situation changed. In the 1970s and 1980s, it became more formalized in state documents. Later, under Kim Jong Il and Kim Jong Un, new interpretations added further layers, like Songun (military-first) or Byungjin (parallel development of nuclear arms and the economy).

- **Kim Jong Il's Role**: As Kim Il Sung's successor, Kim Jong Il wrote extensively on Juche, reinforcing the idolization of his father's thoughts and weaving them into every policy area.
- **Institutionalizing Juche**: Government agencies and research centers were created solely to study and promote Juche. This turned ideology into a kind of state religion.

15.14 Everyday Life Under Juche Influence

For many North Koreans, Juche became the moral and political compass. Social gatherings, family conversations, and workplace meetings all referenced it. Loyalty to the leader and self-reliant thinking were daily themes.

15.14.1 Collective Spirit

Families were told that private ambitions should not overshadow society's needs. Community projects, like cleaning local streets or volunteering extra labor in busy seasons, were framed as living proof of Juche.

15.14.2 Limited Dissent

Over time, the fear of punishment or social exclusion discouraged any open critique of Juche. If a farmer's harvest was poor, they might blame it on bad weather rather than question the system. Public speeches rarely admitted failures, maintaining an image of steady progress.

15.14.3 National Pride

Despite shortages, many North Koreans genuinely felt proud of their perceived independence. They looked at other countries that were heavily influenced by bigger powers and felt that Juche gave their country dignity, especially after a long history of foreign invasions and colonial rule.

15.15 Effects on Society and Government Structure

Juche further centralized power in the hands of Kim Il Sung and the top party elite. The government's structure reflected this:

1. **One-Party Dominance**: All real decisions came from the Workers' Party of Korea, which claimed to embody Juche.

2. **Tight Hierarchy**: Orders moved from top to bottom, with little room for local initiatives unless they matched the official line.
3. **Surveillance and Ideological Control**: A vast security network monitored people for any sign of "anti-Juche" thinking. This kept society rigid and stable, but it also created fear and limited creativity in problem-solving.

15.16 Shifts in the 1970s Economic Push

Fueled by Juche zeal, North Korea in the 1970s attempted grand industrial expansions. Large projects like power plants, steel mills, and chemical complexes were launched.

- **Initial Gains**: Some factories reached high outputs, briefly placing North Korea ahead of the South in certain metrics like steel production.
- **Mounting Debt**: The DPRK borrowed from Western banks as well, hoping to repay with industrial exports. But balancing self-reliance with external loans proved tricky. By the late 1970s, debt problems emerged, though the public remained largely unaware.

15.17 Legacy and Future Directions

Even after Kim Il Sung's death in 1994, Juche lived on as the state's defining ideology. Under his successors, it morphed to justify new policies—like nuclear development and tight border controls. The essence remained the same: North Korea as a closed, self-oriented nation, deeply centered on the Kim family's authority.

15.17.1 Enduring Influence

Today, visitors to Pyongyang see Juche slogans everywhere—on billboards, in schools, even at public squares. The concept still shapes how the government explains decisions, whether it's refusing international aid or celebrating local scientific "breakthroughs."

15.17.2 Debate Among Observers

Some outside analysts view Juche as a propaganda tool that hides the regime's reliance on outside help or black-market trade. Others see it as a powerful national ideology that fosters unity in a country under constant international pressure.

15.20 Conclusion

Juche stands at the heart of North Korea's identity. Rooted in a mix of anti-colonial feelings, socialist ideas, and the determination to break free from Soviet and Chinese influence, it guided Kim Il Sung's leadership for decades. It reshaped politics, culture, education, and foreign relations. On one hand, it gave North Koreans a sense of pride and independence; on the other, it tightened political control and restricted the flow of ideas from outside. Through Juche, Kim Il Sung built a unique socialist state, strengthening the personality cult and setting the stage for future generations of leadership under his family line.

CHAPTER 16

ECONOMIC PLANS AND INDUSTRIAL CHANGES

Introduction

Since its founding, North Korea followed a path of centralized, state-led economic development. Early successes in rebuilding after the Korean War gave confidence to Kim Il Sung and the Workers' Party, who believed they could rapidly transform the country into an industrial powerhouse. In the 1950s and 1960s, the government launched ambitious plans that aimed to surpass even some more developed nations. Backed by the Juche principle of self-reliance, North Korea poured resources into heavy industry, infrastructure, and scientific advancement.

In this chapter, we will examine the evolution of North Korea's economic strategies, focusing on the planned economy system, the role of heavy industry, agricultural management, and trade policies. We will see how some plans achieved early gains, while others encountered serious obstacles. We will also explore how external factors—such as changing relations with the Soviet Union and China, and later, the collapse of the socialist bloc—dramatically impacted North Korea's development path.

16.1 The Planned Economy: Foundations

From the outset, the DPRK chose a Soviet-style planned economy, with state ownership of major resources and detailed five-year (or sometimes shorter) plans that set production targets.

16.1.1 Centralized Decision-Making

Key economic decisions were made in Pyongyang. The State Planning Commission, guided by the Workers' Party, decided how much steel to produce, how many tractors to build, and how many goods each factory or farm needed to deliver.

- **Quotas and Targets**: Each sector—mining, steel, chemicals, textiles—received quotas. Failure to meet quotas was often blamed on poor discipline or lack of ideological commitment, rather than on unrealistic planning.

16.1.2 Early Confidence

In the late 1950s, North Korea's economy grew quickly, thanks in part to reconstruction efforts, external aid from socialist allies, and a low baseline from which to rise. Official propaganda boasted that the north would soon catch up to or even surpass advanced economies. While some of these claims were exaggerated, there was genuine enthusiasm among workers who saw factories buzzing with activity.

16.1.3 Role of the Party

Local factory managers and farm leaders took orders from the party committees. Performance evaluations focused as much on political loyalty as on efficiency. The ideology of Juche infused planning, emphasizing that domestic resources and ingenuity could solve any problem.

16.2 The First Major Plans (Late 1950s to 1960s)

After initial recovery, the government set forth a series of economic plans designed to accelerate growth in heavy industry, while also improving living standards.

16.2.1 The Three-Year Plan (1954–1956)

Shortly after the Korean War, North Korea launched a **Three-Year Plan** to restore industrial output to pre-war levels. It focused on:

- **Factory Reconstruction**: With help from Soviet and Eastern European advisors, major industrial sites restarted production.
- **Agricultural Recovery**: Farmland was cleared of wartime debris, and irrigation networks were repaired.

- **Housing**: Rapid construction of basic housing blocks, especially in Pyongyang.

By 1956, official figures claimed big successes—many sectors reportedly exceeded 1949 output. While the data might have been inflated, there was little doubt that the war's ruins were being cleared at a remarkable pace.

16.2.2 The Five-Year Plan (1957–1961)

This was the first full-scale plan with targets that went beyond mere recovery. It aimed for large increases in heavy industry, particularly steel, coal, and machinery.

- **Speed Battles**: The party urged workers to engage in "speed battles," working extra hours or weekends. Model workers were praised, while lagging areas felt pressure to catch up.
- **Agricultural Cooperation**: Rural cooperatives were expanded, pushing farmers to meet higher grain quotas.
- **Mixed Results**: Some factories did show huge jumps in output, yet agricultural sectors began feeling strain. Shortages of raw materials or skilled technicians occasionally stalled progress.

16.2.3 The Seven-Year Plan (1961–1970)

Originally planned for seven years but extended to 1970, this plan sought to continue heavy industrial growth while also boosting consumer goods to some extent.

- **New Slogan: "Technology First!"**: The government stressed scientific innovation. Research institutes for chemicals, machinery, and electronics were established.
- **Defense Spending**: With the tense atmosphere on the peninsula, a significant share of output went to military-related industries.
- **Infrastructure Projects**: Railways and roads were expanded, though mountain geography made large-scale transport systems costly.

Despite enthusiastic propaganda, many of the plan's goals were not fully met. Official sources still declared victory, attributing any shortfalls to external threats or sabotage.

16.3 Emphasis on Heavy Industry Over Consumer Goods

Throughout these plans, North Korea prioritized heavy industry at the cost of light industry and consumer products. The rationale was to lay a robust industrial base that could, in theory, later provide a higher standard of living for all.

16.3.1 Steel, Machinery, and Chemicals

Steel mills were considered the backbone of modernization. Coal mining expanded, fueling power plants and factories. Chemical plants aimed to produce fertilizers, plastics, and basic pharmaceuticals.

- **Pros**: This focus allowed quick rebuilding of essential sectors after the war. It also supported the military's needs, aligning with defense autonomy under Juche.
- **Cons**: Daily consumer items—like textiles, shoes, soaps—received less attention, leading to chronic shortages. Factories that produced household goods often used outdated equipment or faced supply chain disruptions.

16.3.2 Shortage of Consumer Goods

For the average person, the scarcity of diverse consumer goods meant limited choices. State shops sold uniform clothing, rationed food, and a few household staples. Many families mended clothes for years and reused older items. Authorities praised frugality as a virtue, tying it to the spirit of self-reliance.

16.4 Role of Agriculture and Rural Development

While industry was the main pride, North Korea also understood it needed a stable food supply. After the final push toward cooperatives in the 1950s, agriculture had to keep up with the demands of a growing population.

16.4.1 Collective Farming Strategies

Under collective farming, peasants worked collectively owned land, divided tasks, and shared the harvest according to rules set by the state. Tractors, irrigation systems, and fertilizers were provided by government-run stations.

- **Advances**: Large-scale irrigation projects, mechanization, and new seeds did boost yields at times. Cooperative farms had access to resources that small private farms might not.
- **Challenges**: Rigid quotas led to inflated reports or mismanagement. Peasants felt pressure to meet targets, sometimes resorting to overuse of fertilizer or cutting corners. Poor weather could still devastate entire cooperatives.

16.4.2 Grain Output and the Rice Emphasis

Rice was a major staple, though parts of North Korea's climate and terrain were better suited to maize or potatoes. Officials pushed for high rice yields to match or surpass the south, investing in more irrigation. Results varied. Some coastal plains succeeded, but mountainous areas struggled to meet assigned quotas.

16.5 Balancing Defense and Development

North Korea's security concerns heavily influenced economic decisions. Large sums went into the military sector—developing artillery, small arms, and eventually more advanced weaponry.

16.5.1 Military-Industrial Complex

Certain factories had dual uses: by day they might produce farm machinery, and by night or in special sections, they made military components. Technicians trained in advanced engineering often ended up working in defense-related research.

- **Juche in Defense**: Reflecting Juche, leaders urged domestic production of everything from rifles to submarines. This required specialized materials and technology, straining resources.
- **Tensions with Civilians**: A notable portion of the budget went to defense, so less was left for improving living conditions. Civilian factories sometimes had to wait for spare parts or electricity while defense plants received priority.

16.5.2 The Impact on Everyday Life

With the heightened focus on security, street-level presence of militia units and civil defense drills became common. Citizens got used to regular training sessions, learning how to respond to hypothetical invasions or air raids. The economy was thus shaped by a sense of perpetual readiness for conflict.

16.6 Relations with Socialist Allies and Technology Transfer

In the 1960s and 1970s, North Korea continued to rely on the Soviet Union and China for certain technologies it could not produce itself. However, Kim Il Sung maintained that such help did not contradict Juche, claiming that "mutual cooperation" was different from dependency.

16.6.1 Soviet Technical Aid

Soviet specialists sometimes helped set up modern power plants, steel furnaces, and automotive lines. North Korean engineers traveled to the USSR for training. Despite friction over policy differences, the Soviets remained a vital resource for advanced machinery.

16.6.2 Chinese Influence

China provided cheaper consumer goods and some agricultural machinery. In times of poor harvest, China occasionally sent emergency grain shipments. North Korea reciprocated with coal or minerals. Political ties were complicated by personal differences between Kim Il Sung and Mao, but economic exchanges continued.

16.6.3 Repayment and Debt Issues

By the 1970s, the DPRK owed significant debts to these countries. Paying back was hard because exportable goods were limited. North Korea sometimes tried exporting raw materials or low-end manufactured products but struggled in competitive markets. Over time, default or delayed repayments strained some alliances.

16.7 The "Speed Battle" Campaigns

Throughout the decades, whenever a plan lagged, Kim Il Sung would launch a "speed battle"—a short-term push to energize workers and meet or exceed production targets rapidly. These campaigns aimed to showcase socialist enthusiasm but often led to exhaustion and inefficiency.

16.7.1 Worker Mobilization

Factory managers extended shifts, offered awards, and publicized heroic stories of laborers who "volunteered" to work longer for the collective good. Youth brigades were formed to tackle big tasks such as digging canals or building roads.

16.7.2 Short-Term Gains, Long-Term Strains

While such drives could temporarily boost output, they also wore down machinery and people. Equipment might break under constant operation without proper maintenance. Workers faced burnout, leading to hidden resentment. However, official media praised each speed battle as proof of Juche spirit.

16.8 Modernization Attempts and Emerging Problems

By the late 1970s, the global economy was changing rapidly with new technologies in electronics, computers, and advanced machinery. North Korea tried to keep pace, but its isolation made progress difficult.

16.8.1 Technological Gap

Compared to countries that imported or developed cutting-edge tech, North Korea's isolation put it behind in fields like microelectronics. Factories still relied on older industrial processes. Foreign trade restrictions and limited collaboration with the West contributed to the gap.

16.8.2 Energy Shortfalls

North Korea depended heavily on coal and hydroelectric power. Winter freezes could slow or stop hydro dams, and coal mines sometimes faced disruptions. Electricity shortages became common, slowing production lines and causing blackouts.

16.8.3 Debt and Diplomatic Challenges

Hoping to modernize quickly, North Korea took loans from Western banks in the 1970s. But limited exports and mismanagement led to difficulties in repaying. By the 1980s, some Western creditors labeled the DPRK a credit risk, cutting off further financing. This forced the country to rely more on Soviet or Chinese help.

16.9 Attempts to Improve Consumer Goods

Faced with growing dissatisfaction over consumer shortages, the government made occasional efforts to produce more everyday items—like basic electronics, clothes, and processed foods. But heavy industry and defense typically still won out in resource allocation.

16.9.1 Model Consumer Factories

Some showcase factories, like Pyongyang's textile plants or a few electronics shops, produced TVs, radios, and simple household goods. They were highlighted in propaganda to show that the DPRK cared about people's well-being. However, distribution to rural areas was patchy.

16.9.2 Low Supply, High Demand

Demand for items like bicycles, wristwatches, or even decent shoes often exceeded supply. State stores had limited stock, leading to long lines. Many learned to repair or reuse old items. The party stressed a "selfless, collective spirit," urging patience until the economy matured.

16.10 Comparison with South Korea

In the 1960s and 1970s, South Korea's economy took off under state-led but market-oriented policies. It began producing more consumer electronics and exporting them worldwide. Although direct comparisons were not allowed in the north, some North Koreans secretly learned that the south's standard of living was improving quickly.

- **North's Reaction**: Officials denied these reports or insisted South Korea's growth was for elites only, overshadowed by U.S. exploitation. However, an internal worry grew that the north might be falling behind in some respects.

16.11 Environmental Considerations

As industrial expansion continued, environmental concerns sometimes went overlooked. Factories dumping waste into rivers, deforestation for farmland, and overuse of coal contributed to pollution and land degradation. While not widely discussed, these problems added stress to agricultural capacity and public health.

16.12 The 1980s: Waning Momentum

Entering the 1980s, the global shift in oil prices and the rise of high-tech industries worldwide made it harder for North Korea to keep pace. Soviet support started waning due to their own economic troubles, and China under Deng Xiaoping was moving toward market reforms.

16.12.1 Diplomatic and Economic Isolation

Refusal to open up trade with Western countries or adopt partial market reforms meant the DPRK found itself increasingly isolated. Meanwhile, the south formed trade ties with Japan, the U.S., and eventually other regions, further boosting its economic standing.

16.12.2 Incomplete Reforms

Kim Il Sung occasionally hinted at "new methods" but never embraced large-scale liberalization. Some small pilot programs tested freer trade zones, but they remained heavily controlled. Without a broad policy shift, foreign investment was minimal.

16.12.3 Rising Internal Pressures

Factories that once thrived under central plans now struggled with outdated machinery, lack of spare parts, and limited raw materials. Officials tried to maintain production quotas, but reports of slowdown were common, though rarely admitted publicly.

16.13 The Fall of the Soviet Bloc (Late 1980s to Early 1990s)

One of the biggest external shocks came when Eastern Europe's socialist governments collapsed, and the Soviet Union itself dissolved in 1991. North Korea lost a major trading partner and source of cheap oil, spare parts, and credit.

16.13.1 Immediate Impacts

- **Oil and Fuel Supplies**: Suddenly curtailed, leading to blackouts, halted factory lines, and reduced farm productivity (less fuel for tractors).

- **Loss of Markets**: North Korean products had fewer destinations for export. Payment in rubles or bartering became worthless as the ruble system collapsed.
- **Isolation Grows**: With Soviet support gone, the DPRK had to rely more on China, which was also changing rapidly and less willing to provide unconditional aid.

16.13.2 Adjusting Domestic Plans

Kim Il Sung continued to speak of self-reliance, but the reality was dire. Without external inputs or strong exports, the planned economy faced new crises. Hunger and resource shortages deepened, setting the stage for larger disasters in the 1990s.

16.14 Everyday People and Coping Mechanisms

As industrial and agricultural outputs dipped, many families found alternative ways to survive.

- **Local Barter**: Neighbors exchanged produce, homemade goods, or simple services.
- **Small-Scale Private Plots**: Some were allowed small gardens near homes to grow extra vegetables, a slight concession to practicality over strict collectivism.
- **Unofficial Markets**: Though the state frowned on it, black-market trading emerged. People sold or traded goods smuggled from China or bartered state-provided rations for other items.

16.15 The Legacy of Economic Planning

Despite the problems, North Korea's planned economy did bring some early achievements. It rebuilt the country after war, provided basic social services, and maintained a steady industrial output for a time.

16.15.1 Education and Health Gains

Widespread literacy and an extensive healthcare network were notable positives. For decades, many North Koreans enjoyed a certain level of social security—housing and medical services free at the point of use—though quality varied greatly.

16.15.2 Infrastructure

Transportation and power networks, though not world-class, connected remote regions. Large dams and canals showed the government's willingness to invest in major public works. Monuments and broad boulevards gave cities a distinct, if austere, look.

16.15.3 The Downside of Self-Reliance

Isolation limited technology transfer and global trade benefits. Frequent "speed battles" or unrealistic quotas caused inefficiency. Over time, the system struggled to adapt, especially when the global socialist market collapsed.

16.16 Shifting Paths: Preview of the 1990s Crisis

By the end of the 1980s, cracks were showing. Kim Il Sung's passing in 1994 and the breakup of the socialist bloc left the country in a precarious position. North Korea would soon face a severe food crisis and economic breakdown, leading to mass hardship. Nonetheless, the leadership clung to the Juche approach, further tightening controls.

- **Transition to Kim Jong Il**: Kim Il Sung's son inherited the system, reaffirming the planned economy but adding the "Songun" (military-first) emphasis.
- **Severe Famine**: The mid-1990s saw famine, known locally as the "Arduous March," as foreign aid dried up. This event will be addressed in a later chapter, illustrating the limits of the state's rigid economic policies.

16.17 Reflections on the Planned Economy Experience

Over several decades, North Korea's planned economy showcased both the promise of rapid modernization and the pitfalls of isolation and over-centralization. The system produced some achievements—rapid industrialization in the 1950s and early 1960s—but it also sowed the seeds for future crises.

16.17.1 A High Tide of Ambition

There was genuine optimism in many quarters that socialist planning could outdo capitalist models. Factories ran around the clock, new dams rose on rivers, and literacy soared. Workers felt they were building a society free from exploitation.

16.17.2 Structurally Locked In

As time went by, the inability to adjust plans, encourage innovation, or open up trade stifled growth. Relying heavily on external socialist partners contradicted the Juche rhetoric yet remained essential. When these partners disappeared or cut support, the system faltered.

16.17.3 Social and Political Consequences

The centralization of power in Kim Il Sung's leadership, entwined with Juche, made policy shifts difficult. Admitting mistakes was rare, so problems were hidden under layers of propaganda. This dynamic would carry into the next era, setting the stage for the major challenges of the 1990s and beyond.

16.20 Conclusion

From the post-war rebuilding era to the grand industrial plans of the 1960s and 1970s, North Korea's economy followed a unique path. Shaped by socialist planning, Juche self-reliance, and heavy defense spending, it managed to achieve notable gains early on. However, by the 1980s, signs of stagnation emerged, and the collapse of the Soviet bloc in the early 1990s dealt a severe blow.

These economic changes were closely tied to North Korea's political structure, where Kim Il Sung's decisions guided every aspect of production. While the planned economy helped unify the country around rebuilding efforts and offered some social benefits, it also fostered inefficiency and isolation. In the next chapters, we will see how these economic challenges, combined with leadership transitions and international pressures, led to significant hardships for North Koreans and shaped the DPRK's future course.

CHAPTER 17

CULTURAL AND SOCIAL SHIFTS UNDER KIM IL SUNG

Introduction

By the 1960s and 1970s, North Korea's economic plans and Juche ideology were firmly established. Yet, the story of the country is not just about factories and fields; it also involves the daily lives of ordinary people—how they lived, worshipped, studied, and interacted with each other. Under Kim Il Sung's leadership, culture and society were carefully guided to fit the vision of a unified, loyal population.

In this chapter, we will explore how North Korea shaped its cultural and social environment during Kim Il Sung's era. We will look at how the government approached religion, gender roles, education, family life, and the arts. We will see how traditions were adjusted to emphasize national pride and loyalty to the leader, and how new customs were introduced. Finally, we will consider how regular citizens navigated these policies, sometimes embracing them, sometimes quietly adapting to changes behind the scenes.

17.1 Traditional Influences vs. Revolutionary Change

Korea has a long history that includes Confucian traditions, Buddhism, shamanism, and strong family ties. When the North Korean state formed, it wanted to modernize and cast aside old "feudal" habits. At the same time, it looked to the past for sources of national pride. Balancing these goals shaped the cultural policy.

17.1.1 Confucian Heritage

Historically, Confucian ideas about respect for elders, family hierarchy, and social harmony guided Korean society. North Korean leaders criticized

Confucian "feudal" aspects like rigid class structures, but they also used Confucian values of loyalty, obedience, and group harmony to build a disciplined society.

17.1.2 Buddhism and Folk Beliefs

Buddhism had been important for centuries, and many rural communities practiced forms of shamanism—praying to mountain spirits or household gods. The government viewed such practices as superstitious and unscientific. Over time, many temples were turned into cultural relics or closed. Public shamanic rituals were discouraged. Still, remnants of folk beliefs survived in private, especially in remote villages.

17.1.3 "Revolutionary" vs. "Feudal" Elements

Official slogans distinguished between "revolutionary" culture that supported socialism and "feudal" culture that reinforced old hierarchies. The state systematically promoted or suppressed traditions based on whether they helped unite people under the Workers' Party.

17.2 State Control over Religion

North Korea, following socialist principles, was formally an atheist state. Religion was not outright banned at first, but it was heavily monitored and reduced in influence.

17.2.1 Early Approaches

In the 1950s, some churches and Buddhist temples were allowed to function, though with strict oversight. Certain religious groups even joined official "patriotic" organizations to show support for the new government. Over time, however, these became tokens with little real independence.

17.2.2 Gradual Decline

By the 1970s, most active religious communities had faded. Churches and temples that remained were often used for show—displayed to foreign visitors as proof of "religious freedom." Real spiritual activity went underground or stopped entirely.

17.2.3 Juche as "Spiritual" Fulfillment

Kim Il Sung's government framed Juche as the guiding belief system for the entire nation. The intense devotion required by Juche served much the same role as religion once had—offering unity, moral guidance, and a sense of purpose. Loyalty to Kim Il Sung and the party replaced older religious loyalties for most people.

17.3 Education and Youth Programs

North Korea saw children and young adults as the future of the socialist state. Schools, youth leagues, and cultural programs aimed to shape them into model citizens committed to Juche and the Workers' Party.

17.3.1 The School System

- **Compulsory Education**: Primary and secondary schooling became mandatory. Students were taught a blend of basic subjects—math, science, language—mixed with heavy doses of political ideology.
- **Kim Il Sung Writings**: From an early age, children learned about Kim Il Sung's life and "revolutionary exploits." Textbooks presented him as a near-mythic figure who liberated the nation and guided its progress.
- **Vocational Tracks**: Teens could enter technical schools if they showed aptitude, helping to staff the country's growing industries.

17.3.2 Youth Leagues

Groups like the **Kim Il Sung Socialist Youth League** provided structured activities, from sports to cultural performances. Membership was almost universal. Youth leagues organized mass rallies, volunteer labor, and political study sessions. They instilled discipline, encouraging members to see themselves as "soldiers of the revolution," even during peacetime.

17.3.3 Outside Influences

The curriculum avoided Western culture. Even foreign language classes—if offered—used Soviet or other socialist teaching materials. The goal was to limit outside influence that might contradict North Korean values.

17.4 Family Life Under Socialism

Despite official emphasis on collective spirit, family units remained important in North Korea. However, the state set rules and norms guiding marriage, parenting, and household roles.

17.4.1 Marriage and Courtship

Traditional arranged marriages had been common in Korea's past. Under Kim Il Sung, the state promoted "free choice" marriages, although strong social pressures remained. People were encouraged to pick partners who were good revolutionaries with clean political backgrounds. In some cases, party officials or workplace committees gave "advice" on such personal matters.

17.4.2 Gender Roles

The government proclaimed equal rights for men and women, encouraging women to work in factories or offices. Laws banned arranged marriages and gave women more legal standing. Yet, in practice, many wives still handled home chores while also meeting work quotas. The official line praised women as "flowers of the revolution," but they faced a dual burden of production and reproduction.

17.4.3 Large Families?

In earlier decades, large families were common due to agricultural lifestyles. The government also favored population growth to build a strong workforce. However, space and resources were often limited, especially in cities, so many families settled for fewer children.

17.5 Promotion of Culture and Arts

North Korea devoted significant effort to molding cultural life. Artists, writers, and performers worked under state guidance to create works that celebrated socialist values and praised Kim Il Sung.

17.5.1 The Role of the Party in the Arts

A special bureau within the Workers' Party oversaw literature, music, theater, and film. It decided which themes were acceptable: loyalty to the leader, national pride, love of labor, and hatred of imperialists. Anything else was labeled "anti-socialist" or "decadent."

17.5.2 Revolutionary Opera and Theater

Big, state-sponsored operas like "Sea of Blood" or "The Flower Girl" portrayed heroic peasants or guerrillas fighting for liberation. These productions toured the country, teaching moral lessons about self-sacrifice and praising Kim Il Sung's leadership (often said to have inspired the original stories).

17.5.3 Folk Traditions Recast

Some old folk songs, dances, and tales were adapted to socialist themes. Drums and folk costumes might appear on stage, but the story lines were altered to show peasants rising up against landlords or praising the party. This approach let the state claim a link to Korean heritage while discarding content that clashed with socialist ideals.

17.6 Everyday Entertainment

While official culture centered on grand operas and revolutionary plays, ordinary citizens had smaller forms of entertainment and social life—though all remained under watchful eyes.

17.6.1 Sports and Mass Games

Group sports—football (soccer), table tennis, basketball—were popular. The state hosted occasional national competitions, but mass participation in events like gymnastics festivals was more common. These gatherings showcased discipline, synchrony, and devotion to collective goals.

17.6.2 Radio and Television

Radio was widespread, broadcasting news and music. Most stations repeated official propaganda. Television was limited, mainly in urban areas.

Programming featured educational shows, documentaries glorifying the leadership, or occasionally, foreign films from socialist nations. Strict censorship prevented any Western programs that might challenge the party line.

17.6.3 Social Gatherings

People held small get-togethers for weddings or birthdays, but large private gatherings were discouraged. The government worried that unmonitored groups might spread discontent. Instead, group celebrations often took place through workplaces or neighborhood committees.

17.7 The Concept of the "Model Citizen"

The state created the ideal image of a person who worked tirelessly, studied Kim Il Sung's works, showed unwavering loyalty to the party, and lived frugally. Propaganda stories and films frequently depicted such model citizens—farmers exceeding grain quotas, steelworkers forging record amounts of metal, mothers raising patriotic children.

17.7.1 Labor Heroes and Awards

Workers who surpassed production targets were named "Labor Heroes" and given medals, better housing, or small luxuries. Their images appeared on posters or in newspapers, inspiring others to emulate their sacrifice. This system fostered competition and social recognition tied to political loyalty and production results.

17.7.2 Village and Factory Rallies

When a local factory met or exceeded its quota, officials organized rallies where model workers gave speeches about how Kim Il Sung's leadership motivated them. These rallies reinforced the narrative that success was due to following Juche and the Great Leader's teachings.

17.7.3 Moral Guidance

Through local committees and "criticism sessions," neighbors monitored each other for lapses—like neglecting volunteer work or complaining about shortages. People who stepped out of line might face group scolding, aimed at re-educating them to become a better "socialist person."

17.8 The Role of Women in Society

Officially, North Korea boasted about women's liberation from old feudal constraints. In practice, women still balanced paid work, party activities, and household duties.

17.8.1 Workplace Participation

More women than ever before joined factories, farms, and offices. Some rose to mid-level management or participated in local People's Committees. Laws guaranteed equal pay, though actual implementation varied.

17.8.2 Family Responsibilities

Despite new opportunities, childcare and housework often fell on women. The state tried to help by building nurseries in large workplaces and setting up communal dining halls in some neighborhoods, but resources were limited. Many women struggled with double burdens.

17.8.3 Official Celebrations of Women's Contributions

State media praised "heroic mothers" who raised children to love socialism and simultaneously fulfilled production targets. On International Women's Day, public events honored female labor heroes. Nonetheless, genuine equality remained a challenge.

17.9 Health and Social Services

North Korea claimed to offer free healthcare to all, demonstrating the state's care for the population. While clinics and hospitals existed, actual quality depended on location and resources.

17.9.1 Rural Clinics

In the countryside, small clinics provided basic treatment. Village health workers received short training and handled minor illnesses, referring serious cases to larger hospitals in towns. Modern equipment was scarce, and medicines were often in short supply.

17.9.2 Urban Hospitals

Cities like Pyongyang featured better-equipped hospitals staffed by doctors with some level of formal medical training. However, advanced procedures or specialized drugs were limited. Elite party members sometimes had access to special facilities.

17.9.3 Public Health Campaigns

The government ran vaccination drives, sanitation campaigns, and nutrition programs—especially for children. These efforts reduced infectious diseases, boosting the regime's claim that socialism improved life for everyone, even if not all goals were met evenly.

17.10 Moral and Ethical Framework

In North Korea, the official moral code revolved around collective harmony, loyalty to the leader, and dedication to building socialism. This replaced religious or traditional moralities as the highest guiding standard.

17.10.1 Group Criticism and Self-Criticism

Factories and neighborhood groups held weekly or monthly "criticism sessions." People confessed minor mistakes—like arriving late or missing volunteer projects—while others pointed out shortfalls. The aim was to correct behaviors and prevent private grievances from festering.

17.10.2 The Role of Neighborhood Watch

Each residential block had a local Inminban (people's unit) led by a manager who kept track of every family's comings and goings. This system allowed quick mobilization for mass events, but it also fueled suspicion. If someone missed ideological study, rumors might spread about disloyalty.

17.10.3 Pride in Social Harmony

Propaganda stressed that such systems ensured no one was left behind. North Koreans were told they lived in a society free from crime, unemployment, or exploitation, unlike capitalist countries. Public recognition of wrongdoing was seen as part of the "revolutionary process" to perfect each citizen.

17.11 The Cult of the Leader in Social Rituals

Life events—birthdays, marriages, funerals—often included references to Kim Il Sung and the party. For example, newlywed couples might receive a book of Kim Il Sung's teachings as a wedding gift from their workplace committee.

- **National Holidays**: Days like Kim Il Sung's birthday (Day of the Sun) or foundation dates saw mass celebrations. Families might join parades or spend the day at special exhibits about his life.
- **Memorial Ceremonies**: If a soldier died, the funeral speeches praised the departed's loyalty to Kim Il Sung. This approach strengthened the link between personal milestones and state ideology.

17.12 Shifts in the 1970s and 1980s

Over time, the intense pace of mass mobilizations and ideological events could wear people down. Yet, the government showed few signs of loosening. Instead, under Kim Il Sung's continuing leadership, the daily cultural and social schedule remained packed with volunteer labor days, political study, and patriotic festivals.

17.12.1 A Growing Gap

Some families quietly found ways to enjoy leisure or hold private gatherings, but official policy still insisted on collective spirit. With limited consumer goods, gatherings might revolve around singing patriotic songs or discussing party achievements.

17.12.2 Rising Generations

Younger people, born after the war, knew only this system. Many were sincere in their loyalty. Others, in private, might joke or express minor doubts—but rarely beyond trusted friends or family. A strong security presence discouraged open criticism.

17.13 The Role of Song and Dance in Society

Music and dance were central to North Korean culture, used for both daily enjoyment and grand propaganda events.

- **Revolutionary Songs**: Simple choruses praising the leader or the country. Factories had morning sessions where workers might sing a few lines before starting their shifts.
- **Folk-Inspired Dances**: Choreographers took Korean folk steps and merged them with synchronized group movements. This visually represented the idea of many individuals acting as one under the party's guidance.

17.14 Rural vs. Urban Social Life

In cities, daily life involved large apartment blocks, factories, and offices. In the countryside, cooperative farms dominated life. Nevertheless, the social fabric and cultural norms followed similar patterns.

17.14.1 Urban Apartments

City dwellers lived in apartment complexes built rapidly during reconstruction. Although these buildings were often basic and cramped, families appreciated running water or electricity. Neighborhood organizations arranged regular check-ups on residents' loyalty and well-being.

17.14.2 Rural Village Halls

In farming areas, the village hall served as a hub for meetings, film screenings, and educational sessions. Women gathered for sewing or cooking clubs that also served as chances to share updates on production targets. Electricity and indoor plumbing were less common here than in Pyongyang, reinforcing a sense of difference between rural and urban experiences.

17.15 Women's Groups and Gender Expectations

The **Korean Democratic Women's Union** was a prominent mass organization that mobilized women for farm work, factory production, and political events.

- **Tasks and Training**: The union taught literacy, childcare skills, and party ideology. Women were encouraged to see themselves as both "mothers of the nation" and active socialist builders.
- **Tension with Reality**: While laws promised gender equality, men often had higher positions in management or the party hierarchy. Some women felt pressure to conform to a traditional caretaker role despite official rhetoric.

17.16 Official Attitude Toward Foreign Culture

North Korea's isolation meant limited access to outside music, films, or books. The party worried that foreign ideas could undermine loyalty.

17.16.1 Carefully Selected Socialist Media

Films from the Soviet Union or Eastern Europe were occasionally shown if they met ideological standards. Chinese revolutionary operas also appeared on North Korean stages. Western cultural forms, however, were almost entirely absent.

17.16.2 Controlled Exchanges

Foreign visitors—journalists, diplomats, or allied delegations—were guided on strict tours to see model sites. North Koreans learned that the outside world was full of exploitation and conflict. Only a small number of elite officials had broader knowledge from traveling abroad.

17.17 Fostering Unity and Excluding Dissent

From housing blocks to youth leagues, from women's unions to factories, every sphere of life reinforced a single message: Kim Il Sung and his party know best. This intense cultural and social control aimed to prevent divisions, unify people behind state goals, and maintain stability.

17.17.1 Group Identity Over Individual Expression

In many socialist societies, personal freedom took a back seat to collective goals. North Korea pushed this further than most. Creativity was allowed only within limits set by the party. Self-expression that contradicted official ideology was considered dangerous.

17.17.2 Compliance and Silence

Most North Koreans adapted by conforming. Some believed wholeheartedly in the system. Others quietly followed the rules, avoiding trouble. A minority might harbor private doubts, but fear of punishment kept them silent.

CHAPTER 18

LATER YEARS OF KIM IL SUNG'S RULE

Introduction

Kim Il Sung's tenure as North Korea's leader stretched from the country's founding in 1948 until his death in 1994. While the earlier chapters covered his rise to power, the Korean War, the development of Juche, and massive social engineering projects, we have yet to examine the latter period of his rule—spanning the 1970s to the early 1990s. This phase saw the deep entrenchment of the personality cult, attempts at diplomatic outreach mixed with continued isolation, and the slow emergence of economic strains that would become serious challenges after his passing.

In this chapter, we will explore Kim Il Sung's final decades in power. We will look at how he kept a firm grip on politics, managed relations with foreign countries, and tried to maintain the image of a thriving socialist state. We will also see how the collapse of the Soviet bloc and other global changes impacted North Korea, setting the stage for the crisis that would unfold in the mid-1990s. Throughout these later years, Kim Il Sung remained the central figure in North Korea's narrative—both for successes claimed by state propaganda and for the growing difficulties that lingered beneath the surface.

18.1 Kim Il Sung's Consolidated Power

By the 1970s, Kim Il Sung had eliminated or sidelined all major rival factions. He stood at the apex of the Workers' Party and the government, with no serious opposition.

18.1.1 Party Restructuring

Earlier purges, such as the August Faction Incident (1956), had removed officials who challenged Kim's leadership. By the 1970s, the party hierarchy was filled with individuals loyal to him. Regular party congresses hailed his guidance and reaffirmed Juche as the defining ideology.

18.1.2 Personality Cult Peak

Monuments like the Mansudae Grand Monument in Pyongyang, unveiled in the early 1970s, depicted Kim Il Sung as a giant figure gazing benevolently over the city. Youth organizations, women's unions, and neighborhood committees drilled respect for him into everyday life. The term "Great Leader" (Suryong) became standard in official texts.

18.1.3 Introducing Kim Jong Il

During the 1970s, Kim Il Sung began quietly grooming his son, Kim Jong Il, to take on leadership roles. Kim Jong Il gained control of the propaganda apparatus and cultural affairs, further boosting the elder Kim's image. This set the foundation for a dynastic succession, unusual in communist states but justified in North Korea through the idea of a "revolutionary bloodline."

18.2 Foreign Policy and Diplomatic Shifts

While North Korea maintained its strong rhetoric against "imperialists," it also explored limited diplomacy. Kim Il Sung sought to gain benefits from international relationships without compromising self-reliance.

18.2.1 Cold War Maneuvers

- **Balancing China and the USSR**: Even as relations between Beijing and Moscow soured, Kim remained neutral in public. He extracted aid from both, though less generously than in previous decades.
- **Non-Aligned Movement**: North Korea built ties with countries in Africa, the Middle East, and Asia that were part of the Non-Aligned Movement. It provided some military or technical assistance to friendly states, promoting itself as a model for anti-colonial struggles.

18.2.2 Limited Engagement with the West

In the 1970s and 1980s, some European countries opened diplomatic channels with the DPRK, hoping to reduce tensions. However, Pyongyang's relations with the United States remained hostile. Occasional talks might have occurred through the United Nations or other forums, but no breakthrough in normal relations was reached.

18.2.3 Reunification Proposals

Kim Il Sung often spoke about peaceful reunification with South Korea under a "federal" system, but with strict conditions that would effectively place the south under northern ideology. In the 1970s, there were brief inter-Korean talks, but they stalled as trust was low and each side accused the other of insincerity.

18.3 Economic Challenges Grow

North Korea's planned economy faced obstacles as time went on. Some factories ran on outdated machinery, farmland faced recurring difficulties, and the reliance on Soviet or Chinese resources continued. However, for much of the 1970s, official statements still claimed the nation was forging ahead.

18.3.1 The "Revolutions" in Agriculture and Technology

Kim Il Sung introduced concepts like the "Three Revolutions Movement"—focusing on ideological, technical, and cultural revolutions. Propaganda boasted about breakthroughs in science or new farming methods. In reality, the gains were uneven.

- **Mechanization**: Though tractors and irrigation spread, spare parts and fuel were often short.
- **Use of Chemicals**: Fertilizer and pesticides increased yields for a while, but also led to pollution in some areas.

18.3.2 Debt and Trade Imbalances

To modernize heavy industry, North Korea borrowed from western lenders, anticipating high export earnings to repay. But limited export markets and low product quality caused a trade deficit. By the late 1970s, Pyongyang found itself struggling to service external debts. Eventually, it defaulted on many loans, limiting future credit options.

18.3.3 Quiet Stagnation

While no public admission of recession occurred, many signs showed stagnation: slowed factory outputs, more frequent power cuts, and fewer new buildings. State media continued to highlight achievements and speed campaigns, but the real economy struggled to meet lofty goals.

18.4 Social Life in the 1970s and 1980s

Everyday routines still revolved around collective events. Families rose early for group exercises, students lined up for school assemblies, and workers attended political sessions. However, some subtle changes emerged.

18.4.1 Slight Consumer Improvement

Some attempts were made to produce basic home appliances—like simple TV sets, refrigerators, or fans—for top-performing workers or city residents. These items remained scarce. Owning a black-and-white television became a mark of relative privilege.

18.4.2 Small Modern Touches

In Pyongyang, a few restaurants offered local dishes to families who could afford them on special occasions. Streets had more buses, albeit crowded. Soft drinks or sweets were sold at certain stands, though supply was inconsistent.

18.4.3 Continued Isolation

Travel abroad was reserved for official delegations or elite students. Ordinary people rarely left the country. Domestic travel also required permits. In the countryside, life changed slowly, with cooperative farms continuing their same patterns.

18.5 Heightened Security and Border Controls

The government kept a tight grip on movement and information flow. Fear of infiltration—whether by South Korean agents, Western influences, or disgruntled citizens—remained a major concern.

18.5.1 Militarized Society

Military service was almost universal for young men, and many women also served in some capacity. Regular civil defense drills occurred, training people to respond to hypothetical invasions or air raids. This constant readiness reinforced the sense of being under siege.

18.5.2 Border Zones

Along the northern frontier with China, strict guard posts monitored crossing attempts. Nonetheless, minor cross-border trade or smuggling happened at times, especially in remote river areas. Officially, the regime condemned such activity, but it often served as a vital source of goods for local residents.

18.5.3 Internal Surveillance

The bowibu (security apparatus) and local Inminban committees tracked personal behavior. Citizens complied outwardly, though small acts of quiet defiance—like reading smuggled magazines—might occur discreetly among trusted friends.

18.6 Kim Il Sung's Image as "Eternal President"

As he aged, Kim Il Sung did not relinquish any power. Instead, he expanded ceremonial titles, reinforcing his status as the founder of the nation and father to all North Koreans.

18.6.1 Official Birth Anniversaries

Annual celebrations of Kim Il Sung's birthday, referred to as the "Day of the Sun," became grander. Parades, sports events, and mass performances praised his leadership. City squares displayed huge portraits, while children participated in loyal recitations of his achievements.

18.6.2 Cultural Tokens

Streets and institutions were renamed in his honor. Patriotic songs carried lines about "Kim Il Sung's Korea." Some new housing projects even included mosaic murals of him guiding workers or greeting children.

18.6.3 Preparing the Next Generation

Behind the scenes, Kim Jong Il was increasingly managing state affairs, especially culture and propaganda. Yet all official credit still went to Kim Il Sung, who personified the state and nation. The father-son dynamic was carefully framed as a continuity of the revolutionary lineage.

18.7 Diplomatic Highs and Lows in the 1980s

The 1980s saw notable events in East Asia and worldwide, some of which affected North Korea's position.

18.7.1 South Korea's Rising Status

As South Korea's economy grew and it hosted global events like the 1988 Olympics, its international standing improved. This overshadowed North Korea's image, making Kim Il Sung's claim of the DPRK as the "legitimate" Korea less convincing to many foreign nations.

18.7.2 Attempts at International Outreach

North Korea tried to counter the south's diplomatic wins by fostering ties with Africa, the Middle East, and parts of Asia. It built or funded monuments, offered small-scale military training, and sought new trade deals. Some developing countries saw the DPRK's approach as genuine solidarity, while others viewed it skeptically due to Pyongyang's limited resources.

18.7.3 Incidents and Tensions

On occasion, incidents—like accusations of North Korean involvement in attacks against South Korean officials or foreign nationals—damaged

Pyongyang's global reputation. The U.S. maintained sanctions, further isolating the country. Kim Il Sung blamed "imperialist plots" for these diplomatic hurdles, galvanizing domestic support against external "villains."

18.8 The Sino-Soviet Split's Easing and North Korea's Position

In the mid to late 1980s, the Soviet Union, under Mikhail Gorbachev, began reforms (Perestroika and Glasnost). China under Deng Xiaoping continued market-based reforms. Both countries eased their rivalry. This change challenged North Korea's strategy of playing them off each other.

- **Reduced Tension**: Moscow and Beijing grew friendlier with each other, so Pyongyang couldn't exploit their friction as effectively.
- **Dwindling Aid**: The USSR's economic troubles reduced its ability to give North Korea favorable trade terms. China, now focusing on its own market reforms, was less inclined to provide unconditional support.
- **North Korea's Reluctance**: Kim Il Sung resisted any shift toward market reforms, fearing it would undermine the socialist system and threaten his hold on power. He criticized the Soviet Union's "revisionism" and China's "capitalist tendencies," doubling down on Juche.

18.9 Cultural Projects in the Later Years

Despite economic strain, the government continued staging large-scale cultural spectacles to display unity and power.

18.9.1 The Mass Games Evolution

The Arirang Mass Games, with thousands of synchronized performers forming huge mosaic images, were refined and expanded. They became a key symbol of discipline and collective harmony, with entire stadiums devoted to these events.

18.9.2 New Monuments

Monuments dedicated to the "Three Revolutions" or to Kim Il Sung's alleged battle sites kept appearing. These served as constant reminders of the leader's role in every aspect of national pride.

18.9.3 Artistic Glorification of Juche

Films, operas, and novels continued to glorify Kim Il Sung's biography. They depicted him as guiding the nation from liberation to modernization. Even modest local festivals had to incorporate speeches or images praising him.

18.10 Kim Jong Il's Growing Role

From the late 1970s onward, Kim Jong Il was quietly put in charge of cultural affairs, the media, and eventually the military's political bureau.

18.10.1 The "Center of the Party"

Propaganda began to refer to Kim Jong Il as the "Center of the Party," though not openly naming him as successor. By the 1980s, it was obvious he was being positioned to take over. He perfected the cult of personality surrounding Kim Il Sung, ensuring a smooth transition.

18.10.2 Guidance Tours with Father

Kim Jong Il accompanied Kim Il Sung on visits to factories and farms, learning how to conduct "on-the-spot guidance." Official news praised their teamwork as a sign of stable leadership for the future.

18.10.3 Maintaining Secrecy

Details of Kim Jong Il's personal life remained hidden. The state cultivated an aura of mystery and reverence around him, similar to that of his father.

18.11 Cracks in the System: Emerging Complaints

Though open dissent was dangerous, quiet grumbling about shortages and unrealistic production demands was not uncommon. Some workers noticed the gap between official claims and daily hardships.

18.12.1 Fuel and Power Shortages

Frequent blackouts or factory downtimes harmed productivity. People had to cope with cold winters, using small stoves or limited heating. The party rarely admitted the full scope of these problems, attributing them to sabotage or weather extremes.

18.11.2 Quality of Goods

Clothes and electronics from state factories were often low quality. In contrast, stories of South Korean or Western products, smuggled across borders or shown in glimpses via foreign travelers, hinted at a world of better consumer goods. While these stories weren't widely circulated, they trickled into local rumor mills.

18.11.3 Rural Hardships

Farmers faced tough quotas. During poor harvest years, rations for cooperatives diminished. Some families scavenged wild foods or raised small private garden plots unofficially. Publicly complaining risked being labeled disloyal.

18.12 Diplomatic Brief Flourishes

Occasionally, Pyongyang tried to stage grand gestures to break out of isolation. For instance, in the late 1980s, the regime hosted some international festivals or attempted limited cultural exchanges. But the core isolationist stance prevailed.

18.13 The Fall of the Soviet Bloc and Its Immediate Impact

When communist regimes in Eastern Europe collapsed in 1989, and the Soviet Union dissolved by 1991, North Korea lost critical trade partners and sources of subsidized aid. This represented a seismic shift.

18.13.1 Shock and Denial

North Korean media barely mentioned the changes, or it claimed foreign infiltration had ruined those countries. Kim Il Sung insisted that only "pure socialism" under Juche could survive. Nonetheless, the loss of cheap Soviet oil and machines was devastating.

18.13.2 Searching for New Allies

Pyongyang looked to keep ties with the newly formed Russian Federation, but Russia was less interested in a close alliance without economic benefit. China also pursued its own interests, normalizing relations with South Korea in 1992—an event that Kim Il Sung saw as a betrayal.

18.13.3 Economic Downturn

As external inputs dried up, factories slowed further. Agricultural production faltered without Soviet fertilizers. The state ration system grew strained. People did not starve en masse yet, but the cracks widened, paving the way for a severe crisis in the mid-1990s.

18.14 Kim Il Sung's Final Years

Despite these challenges, Kim Il Sung kept an active public schedule into the early 1990s, touring workplaces, giving speeches, and meeting occasional foreign guests. He projected confidence, though the economy was stumbling and the world around North Korea was drastically changing.

18.14.1 Talks with South Korea

In 1991–1992, there were token inter-Korean contacts. Kim Il Sung said he wanted peace on the peninsula. However, distrust on both sides stalled progress, and the nuclear issue soon overshadowed any chance of real rapprochement.

18.14.2 Preparing for Succession

Kim Jong Il took a more visible role in daily governance. Propaganda hailed him as the "Dear Leader," second only to Kim Il Sung. They were often shown together in photos, signifying a generational handover.

18.14.3 Unexpected Passing

On July 8, 1994, Kim Il Sung died of a heart attack. His death shocked North Koreans, who had been taught to view him as almost immortal. The state declared a long mourning period. Kim Jong Il rose to leadership, but the timing was ominous, given the rising economic crisis and international isolation.

18.15 The Legacy of Kim Il Sung's Rule

When Kim Il Sung died, he left behind a deeply centralized system, a strong personality cult, and an economy that had begun to falter. North Koreans remembered him as the founder of their nation, but also found themselves on the brink of major hardship.

18.15.1 Official Reverence

Soon after his death, Kim Il Sung was declared "Eternal President." His statues, portraits, and teachings remained at the core of public life. The Constitution was even amended to reflect his eternal status, meaning North Korea would always honor him as the guiding spirit.

18.15.2 Mixed Realities

While many older citizens had genuine affection for him, recalling post-war reconstruction and social services, younger generations faced limited opportunities and strict control. The grand achievements often praised in propaganda did not always match daily struggles.

18.15.3 Seeds of Future Crises

Kim Il Sung's policies—particularly the refusal to adapt economically and the reliance on external socialist partners—laid the groundwork for severe trouble once the Soviet bloc disappeared. The system's rigidity made quick reforms or foreign engagement difficult. This would become painfully clear in the mid-1990s famine.

18.16 Life in Transition After Kim Il Sung's Death

Though we will not delve deeply into modern times, it is worth noting that Kim Il Sung's death marked a turning point. Kim Jong Il had to manage the country through widespread famine and further diplomatic standoffs, building on the structures his father had left.

18.16 Cultural Continuity and Change

Even after his passing, the cultural patterns Kim Il Sung had established—mass games, idolization of the leader, tight social control—persisted. Kim Jong Il and later Kim Jong Un followed many of the same templates, ensuring minimal deviation from the father's legacy.

18.17 Conclusion

Kim Il Sung's later years represented both the height of his personal power and the onset of crises that would test the foundations of North Korea. He maintained a firm grip through the personality cult, controlling social life, culture, and politics with little tolerance for dissent. Outside events, however, began to undercut the stable facade—particularly the decline of the Soviet Union and changes in China—which deprived North Korea of vital support.

By the time Kim Il Sung died in 1994, the country was standing at a crossroads. The planned economy was heavily strained, the people's everyday lives were marked by shortages, and international isolation was deepening. Still, his image as the Eternal President lingered, and the social and cultural structures he had built remained largely intact. In the next chapters, we will look at **the challenges North Korea faced before the modern era** and how these final years set the stage for the new leadership and the hardships that soon followed, while still adhering to the spirit and legacy Kim Il Sung had firmly established.

CHAPTER 19

CHALLENGES BEFORE THE MODERN ERA

Introduction

At the end of Kim Il Sung's long rule in 1994, North Korea stood at a crossroads. The economy was strained by the collapse of the Soviet bloc, daily life was difficult for many families, and the country's isolation from the world had grown deeper. Yet, Kim Il Sung's death did not mark a sudden break. His successor, Kim Jong Il, inherited the same structures and doctrines that had defined the nation for decades. Despite lingering problems, North Korea continued along the path set by Juche ideology, state-led planning, and firm control over society.

In this chapter, we will explore how North Korea faced a series of critical challenges before stepping into more recent times. We will discuss the power shift after Kim Il Sung's passing, the severe famine often called the "Arduous March," and the nuclear controversies that shaped Pyongyang's relations with other countries in the late 20th century. While still keeping our focus on history rather than modern events, we will see how these crises tested the resilience of the North Korean system.

19.1 Transition After Kim Il Sung's Death

When Kim Il Sung died in July 1994, many North Koreans were stunned. They had grown up viewing him as their "Great Leader," eternal protector, and father figure. Public mourning ceremonies were large and emotional, with images of weeping citizens filling official media.

19.1.1 Kim Jong Il Takes Control

Kim Jong Il, who had been preparing for leadership behind the scenes, gradually assumed the top positions. He was already the supreme commander of the military and held major party roles. But he did not immediately take the title of President. Instead, Kim Il Sung was declared "Eternal President," and Kim Jong Il became known by titles like "General Secretary" of the Workers' Party and "Chairman" of the National Defense Commission.

- **Maintaining Continuity**: Kim Jong Il promised to follow his father's teachings and preserve Juche ideology. State propaganda presented him as the rightful heir, emphasizing a seamless transition.
- **Mourning Period**: For some time, public events and cultural shows paused or shifted to solemn themes. Citizens were urged to rededicate themselves to the ideals of Kim Il Sung.

19.1.2 No Major Policy Changes

Despite the leadership shift, the new government did not announce sweeping reforms. The economy was already in trouble, and foreign relations were tense, but Kim Jong Il stuck to central planning, strong military focus, and tight social control. This continuity would soon be tested by severe crises.

19.2 The "Arduous March" and Famine

One of the most devastating events in North Korean history unfolded in the mid-1990s, when a combination of factors led to a massive famine. The government later referred to this period as the "Arduous March," linking it to a historical reference of guerilla hardship under Japanese rule, but the suffering was real and widespread.

19.2.1 Causes of the Crisis

1. **Loss of Soviet Support**: After the USSR dissolved, North Korea lost access to cheap fuel, fertilizer, and spare parts. China also reduced its aid, pursuing more balanced relationships, including with South Korea.

2. **Weather Disasters**: Floods and droughts struck in succession, damaging farmland. With fewer fertilizers and broken irrigation systems, harvests collapsed.
3. **Economic Mismanagement**: Central planning struggled to adapt. The distribution of resources was poor, and heavy industry still ate up a big share of the budget, leaving agriculture underfunded.

19.2.2 Collapse of the Public Distribution System

For decades, most North Koreans relied on the state's Public Distribution System (PDS) for food. But as shortages worsened, rations dropped or vanished altogether, especially outside big cities. Rural areas and smaller towns were hit hardest. Many families were forced to forage for wild plants or rely on local barter.

- **Hunger and Disease**: Malnutrition led to weakened immune systems, causing diseases like tuberculosis to spread more easily. In extreme cases, people starved to death.
- **Social Impact**: The famine broke many old routines. Desperate individuals abandoned farms in search of food, or tried to reach nearby towns. Some families split up, hoping that someone could find help elsewhere.

19.2.3 Government Response

Officials did not openly admit a famine. Propaganda mentioned hardships, blaming them on "natural disasters" or "imperialist sanctions." Relief efforts were slow. Neighboring China allowed some cross-border trade, and international aid organizations later tried to assist, but the government carefully controlled where and how aid was distributed.

19.3 Coping Mechanisms and Unofficial Markets

As the formal economy faltered, unofficial markets (called jangmadang) emerged or expanded. In these markets, people traded personal goods or food for anything they needed to survive.

19.3.1 Small Private Plots

Some cooperative farm members secretly grew vegetables on small private patches. Town dwellers might keep rabbits or chickens on balconies, hoping to supplement their diet. Such private efforts were technically discouraged but often tolerated during the famine because they helped reduce unrest.

19.3.2 Cross-Border Activity

In northern border regions, a few people crossed into China to seek food or work. Some returned with rice, flour, or consumer goods. The government tried to stop illegal crossings, but bribery and secret routes became common. This period marked a shift in how some North Koreans viewed the outside world, as they saw glimpses of better supplies just across the border.

19.3.3 Rise of a Grey Economy

Small-scale private trade, once nearly unthinkable in a rigid socialist system, became a survival tactic. Though still risky, these unofficial markets laid early foundations for what would, in later years, become more accepted forms of market activity.

19.4 Party and Military During the Crisis

Kim Jong Il needed support from top officials and the military to maintain stability. He promoted a "military-first" (Songun) policy, prioritizing resources for armed forces even as the civilian population starved.

19.4.1 Songun Beginnings

While Songun is more associated with the post-1990s era, its roots were in the 1990s crisis. Kim Jong Il believed the military was the main pillar of society. Soldiers received more consistent food rations and medical care, ensuring their loyalty and readiness to suppress potential unrest.

19.4.2 Party Apparatus

The Workers' Party remained central but had fewer resources to distribute. Local party officials sometimes made deals with military units or local markets to secure supplies. Propaganda pressed the public to sacrifice for the nation, praising those who "endured even on empty stomachs."

19.4.3 Internal Discipline

State security forces cracked down on any hint of discontent that might spark uprisings. Some people rumored that disgruntled citizens criticized the government, but open protests were rare, given the harsh penalties. Fear, loyalty, and the difficulty of organizing in a controlled environment prevented large-scale revolts.

19.5 Nuclear Tensions Arise

In the early 1990s, suspicions grew that North Korea was pursuing nuclear weapons. This led to a standoff with the United States and the International Atomic Energy Agency (IAEA). While these events foreshadow modern controversies, they also shaped North Korea's late 20th-century outlook.

19.5.1 Suspicion and Inspections

The DPRK joined the Nuclear Non-Proliferation Treaty in 1985, but by the early 1990s, inspectors found discrepancies in the country's declared nuclear materials. The government resisted full cooperation, arguing that they needed a self-defensive deterrent against hostile forces.

19.5.2 The Agreed Framework (1994)

In October 1994, Pyongyang and Washington signed the Agreed Framework, under which North Korea would freeze some nuclear activities in exchange for aid, including light-water reactors and fuel shipments. But the deal soon faced mistrust and delays on both sides.

- **Significance**: This was one of the first direct diplomatic engagements between North Korea and the U.S. At the time, Kim Il Sung had passed away a few months earlier, so Kim Jong Il took responsibility for implementing the agreement.
- **Impact on the Crisis**: Aid from the Agreed Framework might have provided some relief, but it was not enough to fix the broader famine or rebuild the entire economy. Political tensions also overshadowed the possibility of deeper cooperation.

19.5.3 Heightened Sense of Threat

The nuclear issue reinforced the government's claim that external enemies were constantly seeking to undermine the DPRK. Internally, propaganda used the crisis to rally support around Kim Jong Il and the Songun approach.

19.6 Social Shifts During the Late 1990s

Though the famine peaked in the mid-1990s, the aftermath lasted well beyond that period. People's daily habits changed. Some saw the rise of unofficial markets as a partial acceptance of private trade. Others endured deeper isolation in remote areas.

19.6.1 Changes in Family Structures

Tragic losses during the famine broke some families apart. Orphans, known as "kotjebi," wandered cities or countryside looking for food. The state set up some shelters, but resources were limited. Traditional bonds faced strains as survival took priority.

19.6.2 Quiet Erosion of Old Controls

While the government still demanded loyalty, the breakdown of the Public Distribution System meant many people relied on markets or cross-border networks for survival. This shift began to erode the all-encompassing power of the planned economy in everyday life, even if the party still claimed total authority.

19.6.3 Hints of Adaptation

Local officials sometimes turned a blind eye to private trading or small-scale businesses in exchange for bribes or simply to keep social order. This unspoken tolerance indicated that some policies on the ground diverged from central proclamations.

19.7 Relations with South Korea Before Modern Times

Inter-Korean relations fluctuated. In 1991, both Koreas joined the United Nations separately, each recognized internationally as a state. This step was a major symbolic shift.

19.7.1 The Basic Agreement (1991)

The two sides signed the "Basic Agreement" on reconciliation, non-aggression, and exchanges, aiming for gradual improvements. However, the nuclear standoff soon overshadowed these promises, limiting actual progress.

19.7.2 Limited Exchanges

Some small-scale family reunions and sporting exchanges occurred, but they were short-lived. Political tensions, combined with North Korea's famine and internal troubles, made consistent cooperation difficult.

19.7.3 Southern Aid

During the famine, private charities and some South Korean groups tried sending food aid to the north. Officially, Pyongyang claimed such help was not needed, but behind the scenes, certain shipments were accepted, carefully controlled to avoid showing dependence.

19.8 Propaganda in the Late Kim Il Sung Era

Propaganda remained critical. Even as conditions worsened, official media claimed North Korea was successfully following Kim Il Sung's path and that Kim Jong Il was guiding the nation with care.

19.8.1 Eternal Guidance

After Kim Il Sung's death, new slogans emerged about his "eternal presence." The phrase "Kim Il Sung will always be with us" appeared on posters. Kim Jong Il was portrayed as the loyal son continuing the Great Leader's mission.

19.8.2 Explaining the Famine

Official narratives blamed natural disasters and foreign hostility for food shortages. The phrase "Arduous March" linked the crisis to heroic guerrilla struggles, telling citizens to endure hardships as a patriotic duty.

19.8.3 Increased Focus on Military

State-run newspapers and broadcasts praised the army as protectors against foreign invasion. Scenes of Kim Jong Il visiting soldiers or awarding medals appeared often, reinforcing the idea that a strong military was key to survival.

19.9 Cultural Output Despite Hard Times

Even in crisis, cultural events continued. Mass games, revolutionary operas, and giant parades used many resources, but they also boosted the regime's image of unity and resilience.

- **Reasoning**: The government believed that large-scale shows of discipline and happiness would reassure citizens and impress foreign observers.
- **Reality**: Behind the scenes, some performers and participants also suffered from food shortages. But public loyalty displays took precedence over private difficulties.

19.10 Kim Jong Il's Consolidation Before the 2000s

By the end of the 1990s, Kim Jong Il had fully taken the reins, though he did not proclaim himself President; he kept his father as "Eternal President." He exercised control through the National Defense Commission and the party.

19.10.1 Formal Titles

In 1998, the Constitution was amended to reflect Kim Il Sung's eternal presidency, while Kim Jong Il's National Defense Commission chairmanship was described as the "highest post of the state." This arrangement confirmed a unique power structure not found in other socialist countries.

19.10.2 Songun Era Emerges

Military-first policies shaped governance, with resources directed to defense-related industries and the armed forces. Civilian projects took lower priority. This approach mirrored the old system but heightened the army's role even further.

19.10.3 Limited Policy Adjustments

While no grand reforms were announced, there were minor allowances for markets to function, acknowledging that the official ration system had collapsed. Party ideology remained rigid, but local realities forced small deviations.

19.11 External Aid and Changing Attitudes

Desperate for food supplies, North Korea allowed some international aid organizations to operate, though under strict conditions. Foreign workers in these groups saw firsthand the dire conditions in certain regions.

- **Tightly Controlled Access**: Aid groups could distribute food only in approved areas. Government minders accompanied them.

- **Ideological Tension**: Pyongyang was wary that foreign NGOs might spread ideas of liberalism or undermine state authority. Still, the need for relief outstripped these fears.

19.12 Shifts in Mindset Among Citizens

As the famine and economic collapse tested North Koreans' faith in state propaganda, some individuals began questioning official claims. Many still respected the memory of Kim Il Sung but found daily reality far from the promised socialist prosperity.

19.13.1 Survival Above Politics

Hunger overshadowed political ideals for many families. People focused on finding food, whether through small trading, gleaning fields, or bartering. While open dissent was dangerous, the silent priority became basic survival.

19.12.2 Market-Driven Skills

Those with trading or practical repair skills fared slightly better in new unofficial markets. This sparked a subtle shift: economic success depended less on party loyalty and more on entrepreneurial resourcefulness. Still, the state kept an eye on these developments.

19.12.3 Hopes and Fears

Some believed North Korea could recover if the government adapted, perhaps learning from China's market reforms. Others feared that any loosening would invite chaos or foreign exploitation. Officially, Kim Jong Il reaffirmed the Juche line, but behind the scenes, small cracks in total control emerged.

19.13 Diplomatic Thaws and Nuclear Tensions Resurfacing

In the late 1990s, as Kim Jong Il tried to stabilize the country, the nuclear agreement from 1994 began to stall. Aid shipments faced delays, and suspicion grew on both sides.

- **Potential Opportunities**: Some contacts with South Korea hinted at possible dialogues. In 1998, South Korean President Kim Dae-jung proposed the "Sunshine Policy," advocating engagement with the north.
- **Continuing Mistrust**: Hardliners in North Korea saw the Sunshine Policy as a trick, while in the U.S., critics doubted North Korea's sincerity about freezing nuclear efforts.

19.14 Cultural Persistence

Despite everything, the government continued large-scale cultural displays to show unity. Annual events like the Mass Games did not end, even during severe shortages.

- **Reason**: The leadership believed symbols of strength and unity were essential to keep morale from collapsing. Citizens practiced for months in group choreography, pushing the idea that North Koreans still stood together despite hardships.

19.15 Lives of Everyday People in Late 1990s

While city dwellers sometimes had better access to resources (especially in Pyongyang, the showcase capital), provinces lagged. Some families lived day to day on minimal rations, others traveled to find trade opportunities. The gulf between official stories of success and real-life struggle widened.

- **Rural Suffering**: Remote farming communities endured repeated poor harvests, lacking modern equipment or fertilizers. Some farmland had eroded due to deforestation.
- **City Strategies**: Urban residents with relatives in rural areas might barter city goods (like clothing or small items) for extra grains or vegetables grown in the countryside.
- **Social Fabric**: Extended families looked after one another when possible, but widespread scarcity meant not everyone could be saved from hunger.

19.16 The End of an Era, the Start of Another

As the 20th century closed, North Korea found itself battered by famine, overshadowed by nuclear disputes, and struggling to maintain the old systems. Kim Jong Il was in charge, but the memory and image of Kim Il Sung still shaped the nation's identity.

- **Living with Juche**: Official ideology did not change. The leadership insisted that any crisis was due to external foes or natural calamities, never acknowledging flaws in the system.
- **Seeds of Change**: Meanwhile, grassroots market activities signaled the beginning of a slower, more subtle transformation from below.

19.17 Reflections on the Late 20th Century

By the end of the 1990s, North Korea had survived the loss of its founding leader, a devastating famine, and international isolation. The system did not collapse, largely due to the regime's tight control, the fear of alternative options, and the loyalty or resignation of many citizens. However, the years leading up to modern times painted a picture of a country in deep crisis.

19.17.1 Resilience and Regimentation

The state's discipline and propaganda machine kept society from fracturing. People were used to mobilization, group thinking, and closed borders, limiting the spread of dissent.

19.17.2 Eroding Foundations

Underneath, the famine and partial acceptance of black markets revealed cracks in the planned economy. The future viability of strict Juche-based systems was in question.

19.17.3 Setting the Stage for Future Changes

As North Korea stepped into the 21st century, it faced the challenge of sustaining its ideology and leadership structure in an increasingly globalized world. Kim Jong Il would navigate these waters, carrying forward his father's legacy but also dealing with harsh new realities.

19.20 Conclusion

The final decade of the 20th century was a watershed for North Korea. Kim Il Sung's passing, the catastrophic famine, and rising nuclear tensions tested the very foundation of the socialist state. Despite unimaginable hardship, the regime persisted, bolstered by a legacy of centralized power and strict societal control. Unofficial markets emerged as a survival mechanism, hinting that the old rigid order was adjusting—though official policy never admitted it.

As we look forward to the next chapter, **Chapter 20: Steps Toward the Future**, we will see how these pre-modern era challenges shaped North Korea's path into the early 2000s. Though we do not dive deep into very recent events, we can trace how the issues faced during Kim Il Sung's final years and Kim Jong Il's initial leadership cast a long shadow over the nation's future development, diplomacy, and everyday life.

CHAPTER 20

STEPS TOWARD THE FUTURE

Introduction

North Korea's story from ancient times through the 20th century reveals a society shaped by geography, foreign invasions, dynastic rule, colonization, wars, and finally, the communist revolution under Kim Il Sung. As we reach the final chapter of this historical overview, we now consider the steps that lay ahead after the late 1990s. Although we do not dive deeply into modern-day politics or detailed recent events, it is important to connect the past with the outlines of North Korea's path forward.

In this chapter, we will summarize how the nation moved beyond the crises of the 1990s. We will briefly address how the leadership dealt with economic challenges, international isolation, and cultural continuity in the early 2000s and beyond. We will also reflect on the key lessons from North Korea's long history: the role of strong leadership, the power of ideology, and the enduring desire to stand independent. These themes continue to influence the country's approach to diplomacy and domestic policy, echoing the ancient past in modern forms.

20.1 Heritage of Conflict and Independence

From early settlements on the peninsula, Koreans faced invasions and power struggles, forging a cultural identity that valued resilience and pride. Northern territories often saw the rise of strong kingdoms like Goguryeo, shaping local traditions of fortitude. In modern times, this spirit blended with anti-colonial nationalism to create North Korea's unique stance.

20.1.1 Emphasis on Self-Reliance

Throughout history, northern Koreans struggled to maintain control over their lands, whether fighting off Chinese dynasties or Japanese occupiers. This background naturally fed into the modern Juche principle of self-reliance, tying ancient resilience to current ideology.

20.1.2 Historical Claims

North Korea sees itself as the successor to powerful northern kingdoms, referencing Goguryeo or Balhae to assert a proud lineage. Textbooks highlight these ancient states' achievements, linking them to modern national pride.

20.2 The Kim Family Legacy Continues

After Kim Il Sung's death in 1994, Kim Jong Il guided the country, followed by Kim Jong Un in the 21st century. The Kim family's hold on power is deeply intertwined with the narrative of historical continuity and Juche.

20.2.1 The "Paektu Bloodline"

State propaganda speaks of a "Paektu bloodline," claiming the Kims originate from the sacred Mount Paektu region. This mythic image supports their right to rule. While many outside observers question these stories, they hold strong symbolic weight at home.

20.2.2 Shaping Leadership Style

Kim Jong Il formalized Songun, elevating the military's role. Kim Jong Un, who took over in late 2011, continued the tradition of on-the-spot guidance, factory visits, and controlling the narrative. Even with some policy changes, the main structure—one supreme leader, supported by a devoted party—remains intact.

20.3 Economic Adjustments in the Early 21st Century

Facing lingering challenges, North Korea made limited economic shifts, though always under tight state oversight. Small market spaces, once purely illegal, became semi-official.

20.3.1 Market Tolerance

After the famine, the government realized that unofficial markets helped provide goods. While suspicious of capitalist influence, they allowed some regulated "farmers' markets," where people sold surplus produce or consumer items. Over time, these markets grew in scope and importance.

20.3.2 Special Economic Zones

North Korea tried setting up special economic zones (e.g., the Rajin-Sonbong area) to attract foreign investment. Results were modest, largely due to sanctions, limited infrastructure, and Pyongyang's cautious approach. Nevertheless, such zones signaled the regime's awareness of global economic realities.

20.3.3 Mixed Success

Although some partial reforms helped ease shortages, the core planned system remained. Officially, North Korea insisted that Juche socialism was still supreme. The reliance on these small openings underscored the struggle to sustain the older model on its own.

20.4 Diplomatic Ebbs and Flows

In the early 2000s, the nuclear issue resurged, leading to multi-nation talks. Periods of tension and partial agreements alternated, reflecting a pattern inherited from late 20th-century standoffs.

20.4.1 Six-Party Talks

For a time, North Korea engaged in discussions with South Korea, the U.S., China, Russia, and Japan, seeking security guarantees or aid in return for limiting nuclear activities. The talks produced some statements but did not achieve lasting resolution.

20.4.2 Occasional Engagement

Certain years saw warmer inter-Korean moments, including summits between leaders of the north and south. Cultural exchanges, tourism projects like Mount Kumgang, and family reunions offered hope for reconciliation. However, changes in leadership, external pressures, or nuclear disputes often disrupted progress.

20.4.3 Sanctions and Isolation

As nuclear tests occurred in the 2000s, international sanctions tightened, restricting trade and finance. North Korea denounced such measures as attempts to force regime change, justifying continued defense buildup under Songun or later policies.

20.5 Cultural Consistency

Despite some economic and diplomatic fluctuations, North Korea's cultural life still mirrored traditions set under Kim Il Sung: mass games, idolization of the leader, and group mobilization.

20.5.1 Updating Propaganda

Modern touches appeared in state media, such as computer graphics or carefully produced TV segments. Yet the core message—loyalty, Juche, threat from foreign powers—remained the same, building on decades of established storytelling.

20.5.2 Technology and Censorship

A restricted intranet emerged, offering official content within North Korea. Access to the global internet stayed limited and closely monitored, preventing free flow of outside information. The regime's tight cultural control, developed long ago, adapted to new communication tools.

20.6 The Historical Thread: Key Lessons

Looking across North Korean history, several themes stand out, guiding the country's steps into the future:

20.6.1 Resilience and Central Control

From ancient kingdoms to post-Korean War rebuilding, northern communities valued strong leadership and collective discipline. Modern North Korea, under the Kim family, took this trait to an extreme, centralizing all power at the top.

20.6.2 Isolation vs. Influence

Historically, northern states balanced between outside interactions and guarding their autonomy. The DPRK continued this pattern by limiting foreign contacts, yet still relying on aid or trade in times of need.

20.6.3 Ideology as Glue

Throughout centuries, various beliefs—Confucianism, Buddhism, folk traditions—shaped culture. In the modern era, Juche replaced them all, providing a unifying principle that demanded loyalty and explained all hardships as part of a larger struggle.

20.7 Possible Paths Ahead

Though we avoid diving into very recent or ongoing events, it is clear that North Korea's future decisions will be influenced by the same historical forces:

1. **Economic Balance**: Whether the country loosens state controls or continues central planning will reflect how well it manages to feed and house its people.
2. **Diplomatic Isolation vs. Engagement**: The question of how much to open up, either to South Korea or the wider world, remains central. Past patterns suggest a cycle of negotiation and conflict.
3. **Leadership Continuity**: With the Kim dynasty firmly in place, leadership transitions are likely to follow the established family lineage. Public loyalty to the Kim family remains an official hallmark.

20.8 Cultural Preservation and Change

North Korea's culture draws from a deep well of Korean traditions, reinterpreted through socialist and Juche lenses. Going forward, the tension between preserving older ways, continuing the personality cult, and adapting to modern ideas will shape social evolution.

20.8.1 Monuments and Memory

Huge monuments to Kim Il Sung and Kim Jong Il will likely stand for generations, cementing their place in national memory. School lessons will continue praising their achievements, keeping the official version of history alive.

20.8.2 Generational Shifts

Younger people, exposed to limited foreign media or hearing stories from relatives who have traded across borders, might gradually question older narratives. Whether they can openly express these thoughts depends on how the leadership manages social controls.

20.9 Potential for Inter-Korean Relations

Given historical patterns, we can guess that relations between North and South Korea might see sporadic improvements—like joint projects or family reunions—followed by setbacks if political or military tensions spike.

- **Historical Roots**: Both sides claim to seek reunification, but with vastly different systems. Centuries of a unified peninsula still echo in shared language and culture, but the divide has hardened over decades of separate governance.
- **Dream of Unity**: Past attempts at dialogue highlight a lingering hope for eventual peace. The shape of such unity, if it ever comes, remains uncertain.

20.10 Reflecting on North Korea's Long History

From ancient tribal settlements to dynastic states, from colonial domination to a socialist revolution, North Korea's past is rich and complex. The 20th century saw the rise of a one-party system around Kim Il Sung, the ravages of war, rapid rebuilding, and eventual stagnation. Through it all, the people's experiences have ranged from hardship to pride, shaped by the interplay of geography, foreign powers, and powerful internal leadership.

20.10.1 A Distinctive National Identity

Geographic isolation, plus the emphasis on unique ideology, created a society that views itself as special and self-reliant. This identity has roots in older kingdoms but was transformed under communist rule, forging a culture of loyalty and discipline.

20.10.2 Strengths and Vulnerabilities

North Korea's system has displayed remarkable endurance, surviving warfare, famine, and sanctions. However, its closed nature and dependence on external aid during crises highlight ongoing vulnerabilities.

20.11 The Role of History in Shaping the Future

Leaders in Pyongyang often use history as a tool—to claim they are continuing the legacy of ancient heroes or fulfilling Kim Il Sung's mission. Ordinary citizens, too, draw lessons from the stories of past resilience.

- **Historical Memory**: Grand monuments and state propaganda keep the memory of Kim Il Sung's era alive, reminding everyone of the sacrifices made.
- **Potential Shifts**: If the state chooses to adapt, it might selectively reinterpret history to justify new policies. Conversely, if it remains rigid, history will continue to be taught as a straight line from Goguryeo to Kim Il Sung to the present.

20.12 Closing the Book on Past Conflicts

While we cannot detail modern times, we can see how the old conflicts—like the rivalry with South Korea, the memory of Japanese occupation, and suspicion of Western powers—still color North Korea's worldview. The multi-chaptered story of invasions and wars in the peninsula fosters a deep national desire for security and autonomy.

20.13 Education and Propaganda Looking Forward

Future generations in North Korea may continue learning about Gojoseon, Goguryeo, and Joseon, all culminating in the Kim family's rule. The carefully curated historical timeline underscores the theme of a nation always defending its sovereignty, whether against ancient invaders or modern pressures.

20.14 The Kim Dynasty's Lasting Influence

Since Kim Il Sung's time, the Kim dynasty has been woven into every aspect of North Korean life—politics, culture, ideology, and even the constitution.

This dynastic system is both a continuation of older Korean royal traditions and a unique invention of socialist monarchy. Whether it changes or endures in the future remains a major question.

20.15 Society's Adaptations

Over centuries, North Koreans adapted to many changes: from tribal life to kingdoms, from monarchy to Japanese rule, and from colonial liberation to a highly centralized socialist state. Today's challenges might spur further adaptations—perhaps bigger market activity or new forms of diplomacy—though under tight state oversight.

20.16 Global Context and North Korea

Looking at the long arc of Korean history, North Korea's global situation is unusual—one of the few remaining states that emerged from the early Cold War era and kept its ideological structure intact. As global forces evolve, North Korea's leadership will either adapt or find itself constantly defending the old system.

20.17 Summing Up Key Historical Themes

Before we conclude, it's worth restating some major lessons from the entire sweep of North Korean history:

1. **Geographic Determination**: The mountainous, resource-rich north shaped people's hardiness and influenced their strategies for defense and trade.
2. **Influences of Mighty Neighbors**: From ancient times to the modern era, China and other regional powers left marks on politics, culture, and survival strategies.

3. **Powerful Central Authority**: Whether under dynasties or the socialist regime, strong leadership and central control characterized northern governance.
4. **Culture as Control**: Arts, religion, and social life often served to unify the populace under a dominant ideology, from Confucian rules to socialist Juche.
5. **Resilience Through Hard Times**: War, famine, isolation—North Koreans repeatedly adapted to crises, though often at great human cost.

20.18 Conclusion

North Korea's long history—from early settlements to the end of the 20th century—reveals a place shaped by rugged geography, deep historical pride, strong central rule, and a determination to be free from outside control. Under Kim Il Sung, North Korea built a highly centralized socialist system anchored in Juche ideology. The country experienced war, rapid reconstruction, significant achievements in social services, and later, crippling shortages and famine.

As we close this book, we leave North Korea on the cusp of the 21st century, wrestling with the legacy of its founding leader, the aftermath of the "Arduous March," and the uncertain global environment. While we have not delved into recent years, it is clear that North Korea's future will continue to be influenced by the same forces that guided its past: the interplay of strong leadership, the pursuit of self-reliance, the push and pull of foreign relations, and the unyielding resilience of its people. The final chapters of North Korea's story remain unwritten, but the lines drawn by centuries of struggle, tradition, and transformation will keep guiding its steps toward whatever future may unfold.

Help Us Share Your Thoughts!

Dear reader,

Thank you for spending your time with this book. We hope it brought you enjoyment and a few new ideas to think about. If there was anything that didn't work for you, or if you have suggestions on how we can improve, please let us know at **kontakt@skriuwer.com**. Your feedback means a lot to us and helps us make our books even better.

If you enjoyed this book, we would be very grateful if you left a review on the site where you purchased it. Your review not only helps other readers find our books, but also encourages us to keep creating more stories and materials that you'll love.

By choosing Skriuwer, you're also supporting **Frisian**—a minority language mainly spoken in the northern Netherlands. Although **Frisian** has a rich history, the number of speakers is shrinking, and it's at risk of dying out. Your purchase helps fund resources to preserve and promote this language, such as educational programs and learning tools. If you'd like to learn more about Frisian or even start learning it yourself, please visit **www.learnfrisian.com**.

Thank you for being part of our community. We look forward to sharing more books with you in the future.

Warm regards,
The Skriuwer Team

www.ingramcontent.com/pod-product-compliance
Lightning Source LLC
LaVergne TN
LVHW012036070526
838202LV00056B/5514